COUNTERPOINT
EXPLAINED

BY DAN MASKE

To access audio, visit:
www.halleonard.com/mylibrary

Enter Code
1169-3073-9476-6674

ISBN 978-1-5400-8801-7

Visit Hal Leonard Online at
www.halleonard.com

World headquarters, contact:
Hal Leonard
7777 West Bluemound Road
Milwaukee, WI 53213
Email: info@halleonard.com

In Europe, contact:
Hal Leonard Europe Limited
1 Red Place
London, W1K 6PL
Email: info@halleonardeurope.com

In Australia, contact:
Hal Leonard Australia Pty. Ltd.
4 Lentara Court
Cheltenham, Victoria, 3192 Australia
Email: info@halleonard.com.au

CONTENTS

INTRODUCTION

While *counterpoint* literally means "point against point" (or "note against note"), the term has come to mean the practice of combining two or more *different* melodic lines in a musically satisfying way. Counterpoint is not two or more parallel lines, like in a lot of pop/rock vocals. Traditional counterpoint sees two or more simultaneous melodic lines, where all lines hold up on their own, as interesting melodies. If you're looking to create a certain sophistication to your composition, traditional counterpoint can sound complex, interesting, and even clever. A listener might ask, "How did the composer get multiple interesting melodies to work together so well, without occasionally clashing?"

If we extend the definition of counterpoint, it may describe any two or more simultaneous melodic lines. This might include a melodic theme against a bass line, or a vocal melody against a guitar riff in a rock song, where one of the lines is more supportive of the other. Even though traditional counterpoint maintains that both lines are of nearly equal importance, this expanded definition allows for one of the lines to be subordinate to the other. In these cases, it still takes thought and planning to make sure both lines work well together. With these considerations, counterpoint doesn't have to sound particularly busy or sophisticated, and is certainly not limited to classical music. Many of the same principles of traditional counterpoint still apply, and thus being well versed in these principles means you can make use of them, in almost any style of music.

This book will cover traditional counterpoint, then step outside of this and present a variety of situations where two melodic lines are at play simultaneously. There will also be sections of this book dedicated to *when* and *why* a composer might wish to employ counterpoint. These discussions will cover multiple styles of music.

Counterpoint has several purposes. It can:

- Add interest to a melodic line, as opposed to thickening the melody with other lines that have the same rhythm and contour.

- Aid in the development of melodic themes, by providing the opportunity to sound multiple melodies at the same time.

- Create a thick and full texture with something besides chords.

- Cover a lot of territory with just two single-note instruments (e.g., flute, trumpet, or voice, as opposed to piano or guitar).

With one of the major challenges of counterpoint being the avoidance of undesirable clashing sounds (dissonance), much of what will be covered involves intervals, and how to write in a way that avoids intervals that clash, or at least avoid clashing in inappropriate places. However, counterpoint is about more than simply avoiding clashing dissonances. Music isn't about being correct, as in a science or math. Carefully working out two different lines so that nothing sounds "wrong" is only part of the objective, and arguably, not the main part. Just as performing a piece of music accurately does not make it a great performance, writing counterpoint avoiding anything that sounds "bad" doesn't necessarily make for good counterpoint. A composer wants to achieve these things, while also creating something special, unique, interesting, catchy, all the above, and more. Sometimes, something that may not be "correct," in that it breaks a rule of traditional contrapuntal technique, is just what the music needs to make it special. Imperfections which work in mysterious and almost magical ways are what makes music special and qualify it as an art.

RULES AND TRADITIONAL TECHNIQUES

You are going to see the word "rules" used a lot in this book. This term is used to describe characteristics that make for good counterpoint, according to traditional practices that are a part of much of the great music from the past few hundred years. You might be telling yourself you don't wish to follow rules, as doing so will make you sound like everybody else, that breaking rules seems more adventurous and artistic, and can help your music be more unique. You would not be wrong in this. However, rules can be used as a guide, a way for you to help achieve the sounds you desire. If you've composed music already, you know that there are plenty of times when you create something such as a melody, and while you like it, you're not totally happy with it. Something sounds a bit off. Knowing traditional rules can help you identify what might not be sitting right with your ears. You can use these rules to help enhance any moments where the music is not achieving what you want.

Rules do have their place, and many composers create music, following a specific set of rules without realizing it, because the rules have become engrained. It is common for a young composer to see rules as something restrictive, and they claim they don't want to be limited by rules. But then they compose a piece in the key of C minor, using four different chords, with two verses, two choruses, and a bridge. Without realizing it, they've followed a strict set of rules. Part of composing is learning certain rules and traditions, and then learning what you can do within those boundaries. With experience, you'll learn that these boundaries are not very restrictive, and can often help shape and improve your raw creative ideas.

While this book uses the principles of traditional classical counterpoint as a foundation, it also demonstrates how counterpoint plays an important role in popular music in a variety of styles. One traditional method of writing counterpoint is with the use of an approach called *species counterpoint*. This contrapuntal method originates back to the early 18th century. However, even though the approach dates back almost 300 years, its principles helped guide many of the famous classical composers we know today, as well as many forms of modern popular music. This book will take a complete look at species counterpoint, illustrate how it manifested itself in classical music, and then show some practical use for it in pop/rock music of today.

You will learn that species counterpoint is based on doing five types of exercises, where you are writing counterpoint under strict rules. To a composer, doing species counterpoint exercises is like playing scales to a performer. Scales can be used as a warm-up, to develop tools for improvisation, and to get you familiar with playing in different keys without having to constantly be on the lookout for which notes are to be played flat or sharp. For a composer, writing species counterpoint helps warm up the creative brain of the composer, developing the use of certain counterpoint writing tools as something that comes automatically. Composers will have certain contrapuntal concepts memorized and will have developed an ear for hearing contrapuntally (in other words, noticing when something in two melodic voices doesn't quite work, as well as when something works beautifully). One can also take a species exercise and turn it into "real music."

Rather than creating one melody, and harmonizing it with chords (referred to as homophonic music), some counterpoint involves creating an accompaniment to a melody with another melody (referred to as polyphonic music). In some cases, neither melody is viewed as the main melody nor the countermelody. Multiple melodies may be created simultaneously, where creating notes for one melody helps shape creation of the other(s). But in a lot of modern popular music, one melody is created first, and serves as the main melody, while the other melody is created to serve and support the first.

Take any two melodies that are in the same key and meter and play them at the same time as each other. How does it sound?

 Track 1

Notice that it sounds like there are wrong notes in a couple spots; in other words, some things seem to be clashing. These clashes are *dissonances*. But the incorrect sound is not due to the simple fact that they are dissonant rather, where they are, how they are approached (what comes right before them), and how they are resolved (what comes right after them). In addition, good counterpoint involves each melodic line having its own, distinct rhythm. In the first bar, both melodies have the same rhythm. In counterpoint, we usually want them to be at least a little different from each other.

Counterpoint is "compositional," meaning it isn't something where both/all melodic lines can be improvised, at least not by two different players. If you are tasked with creating a countermelody to another existing melody, it is possible to improvise your countermelody if you know the existing melody well. But two players, both improvising lines at the same time, cannot create something together which is purposefully contrapuntal. This means that the two melodies are probably contrasting from each other, and don't work together very well. Counterpoint is most effectively created through notation, as opposed to trying to create two or more lines, entirely by ear (this is done, especially in the case of rock/pop bands without music reading ability. It can take much longer to achieve compared to writing the counterpoint down). Notating the musical lines on the staff allows the composer to see the possibilities carefully and easily, as the written notes are frozen in time.

PART ONE:
FOUNDATIONAL COUNTERPOINT CONCEPTS

CHAPTER 1: INTERVALS

Counterpoint requires careful, precision composing, and knowing your intervals inside and out will be useful in composing counterpoint precisely. This chapter provides the basics on intervals. To take these basics and turn them into skills you can use quickly, you are encouraged to study and practice them using flashcards to drill their notation, as well as engage in ear training working on how you hear them.

At the most basic level, counterpoint is about two things: 1. Creating melodies and 2. The interaction between two or more melodies, sounding at the same time. This second item, when referring to the "interaction," we are talking about the intervals between any notes sounded at the same time.

An interval is the distance between two pitches. There are two elements used in determining a complete identification of an interval: *interval size* and *interval quality*. In addition, an interval may be described in terms of being either *consonant* or *dissonant*.

INTERVAL SIZE

When attempting to identify an interval, the first step is to determine the *interval size* (sometimes referred to as "arithmetic distance"). This is done by counting the letter names of the two pitches which we are trying to find the distance of, plus the letter names in between. For example, when considering A up to B, "A" is one and "B" is two, thus this distance is a 2nd. Similarly, A up to C would be a 3rd ("A" is one, "B" is two, and "C" is three: 3rd), and A up to E is a 5th.

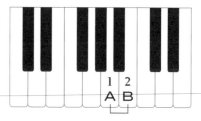

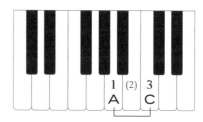

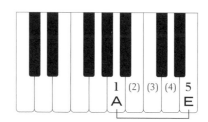

INTERVAL QUALITY

To more completely identify an interval, one must also determine the *interval quality*. For the purposes of counterpoint, interval quality is less important. For example, whether something is a major 3rd or a minor 3rd usually does not matter. However, the following will help to get you well versed in intervals, which can come in handy for a variety of musical purposes.

As illustrated in the previous example, an A up to C is a 3rd, but what type of 3rd is it? If you refer to the piano keyboard, you'll notice that in counting all keys, black and white, A up to C, a 3rd, encompasses three half steps (A up to B♭ is one, B♭ up to B is two, and B up to C is three). While if we consider C up to E, also a 3rd, this distance encompasses four half steps. Both intervals are 3rds, but we must have a way to differentiate between these two types of 3rds, as they are in fact different distances. Thus, we have different interval qualities, such as *perfect*, *major*, *minor*, *diminished*, and *augmented*.

PERFECT

The intervals of the unison, 4th, 5th, and octave are the only four intervals that can be labeled "perfect." In the Medieval and Renaissance periods, these were the only intervals considered appropriate for places of rest or resolution, such as the ending of phrases. Thus, the label "perfect" was used to describe these intervals.

To figure out these perfect intervals, one might count the number of half steps, use the major scale, or both. In cases of uncertainty, where you wish to check your work, it may be beneficial to use both methods. For example, a perfect 5th consists of seven half steps. G is seven half steps above C, thus a perfect 5th. However, it is important to make sure to have the correct interval size; in other words, the correct letter names. B up to F♯ is seven half steps, but so is B up to G♭. But B to G♭ is not a fifth, rather, it is a 6th.

An octave is perhaps the simplest interval to use to demonstrate this important detail. C♯ up to the next C♯ is an octave (a perfect octave, to be precise). But although D♭ up to C♯ involves the same two pitches as C♯ up to C♯, we cannot call this an octave, because an octave must have the same two letter names. Consider the 2nd, an interval we know to consist of two adjacent letters in the alphabet. C♯ up to D♯ is a 2nd. But C♯ up to E♭ is not, rather it is a 3rd. Spelling matters, and it matters in a variety of ways that have to do with musical context. To learn more about this musical context, further study on intervals is recommended, beyond what is necessary for the purposes of this book.

The other method that can be used to measure perfect intervals is to apply the major scale. (See Chapter 3 for a complete discussion of scales). In a major scale, the first degree (1) up to the 4th degree (4) is a perfect 4th (P4), and 1 to 5 is a P5.

MAJOR

Counting half steps and/or using the major scale can be used to measure *major intervals*. The major scale, from the 1st degree to the 2nd, 3rd, 6th, and 7th degrees are all major intervals (2nd, 3rd, 6th, and 7th, respectively).

The following chart uses the C major scale to show the number of half steps that each of these major intervals span.

SCALE DEGREES	PITCHES	NO. OF HALF STEPS	MAJOR INTERVAL
First to Second	C up to D	Two	Major 2nd
First to Third	C up to E	Four	Major 3rd
First to Sixth	C up to A	Nine	Major 6th
First to Seventh	C up to B	Eleven	Major 7th

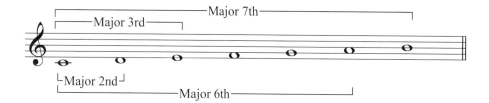

MINOR

Some musicians prefer to use major scales, major chords, and major intervals as a reference point to figure out those that pertain to minor. Having these "major" elements memorized means one can quickly get to anything minor. For example, if you know that C up to E is a major 3rd, you can lower (or shrink) the interval by a half step to turn it into a *minor interval*. Remember, you must maintain the same two letter names. So, lowering the E to E♭ gives you C up to E♭, which is a minor 3rd.

DIMINISHED

Diminished intervals are one half step smaller than their minor or perfect counterparts. For example, C up to E♭ is a minor 3rd, so C up to E♭♭ is a diminished 3rd. Or, turn the C into a C♯, and C♯ up to E♭ is a diminished 3rd. It's the equivalent of two half steps (or, a whole step), but since the spelling involves two letter names with one letter between them (D), it's still identified as a 3rd rather than a 2nd.

Any perfect interval which is made smaller by a half step becomes diminished. C up to G is a perfect 5th, but change the G to a G♭, and it becomes a diminished 5th. Any minor interval made smaller by a half step becomes diminished.

The following chart shows all diminished intervals starting from A, including the number of half steps that span each distance. The chart takes the minor and perfect intervals that occur from the first degree of the A natural minor scale.

SCALE DEGREES	ORIGINAL PITCHES	MINOR INTERVAL	PITCHES WHEN SHRUNK BY HALF STEP	DIMINISHED INTERVAL
First to Third	A up to C	Minor Third	A up to C♭	Diminished 3rd
First to Fourth	A up to D	Perfect Fourth	A up to D♭	Diminished 4th
First to Third	A up to E	Perfect Fifth	A up to E♭	Diminished 5th
First to Sixth	A up to F	Minor Sixth	A up to F♭	Diminished 6th
First to Seventh	A up to G	Minor Seventh	A up to G♭	Diminished 7th

Some of the spellings may look strange to you, especially those where double flat symbols are used. While the diminished 5th and diminished 7th often may be found in music, the other diminished intervals are not commonly seen.

AUGMENTED

Taking a major or perfect interval and increasing the distance by one half step results in an *augmented interval*. As always, remember that the letter names must remain the same. Meaning, if C up to G is a perfect 5th, then spelling an augmented 5th up from C results in a G♯ and not an A♭. C up to A♭ would be a 6th. Similarly, the major 3rd of C up to E becomes an augmented 3rd when the E is raised to E♯. [Even though one would commonly see this distance spelled as a C up to F (a perfect 4th).] There are cases where the musical context (largely having to do with the key of the music) requires that this F be spelled as an E♯. Think of words that sound the same, but are spelled differently (e.g., "night" and "knight"). If someone were to simply say "night," but not as part of a sentence, you wouldn't know the meaning of the word. But used in a sentence such as, "The knight drew her sword, getting ready to defend herself," it becomes clear why this word needs to be spelled as "knight," even though "night" may be easier to spell. The same is true for music. For a more detailed examination on the topic of spelling notes in relation to their musical contexts, it is suggested you take on a more expansive study of music theory.

For now, study the following chart, which shows augmented intervals, starting on C, along with the number of half steps of which each interval consists.

CONSONANCE AND DISSONANCE

With respect to counterpoint, we are usually referring to *harmonic intervals*; the distance between two pitches, which are sounded at the same time. The terms *consonance* and *dissonance* are used to characterize harmonic intervals as being either stable (consonant) or unstable (dissonant). This is *very* important to counterpoint!

Whether a certain interval is considered consonant or dissonant depends on the context, not only in the music at hand, but also in historical context. The concept as to which intervals are considered consonant and dissonant is a generally accepted among a wide variety of musical styles.

CONSONANCES

Consonant intervals sound stable. They don't sound as if there were tension or clashing producing the need to resolve to a different interval. The consonant intervals are the P1 (P = perfect), m3 (m = minor), M3 (M = major), P5, m6, M6, and P8. Consonances may be divided into two types: perfect and imperfect.

- Perfect: P1, P4*, P5, P8

- Imperfect: m3, M3, m6, M6

  *The perfect 4th is sometimes considered a dissonant interval, depending on how it is used, something that will be covered later.

Perfect consonances sound open and completely at rest, whereas imperfect consonances have more tension to their sound. With perfect consonances, it can sometimes be difficult to tell when two notes are being played at the same time as opposed to just one.

DISSONANCES

Dissonant intervals sound unstable. They provide the necessary tension in the harmony, pushing the music forward, providing for the sensation of resolving. Dissonant intervals include the m2, M2, tritone (augmented 4th or diminished 5th), m7, and M7. These intervals sound as if they need to resolve. However, in certain music, such as 20th century classical music as well as modern film music, dissonance if often used as an effect. Playing many dissonances that do not resolve, can establish a certain mood or emotional quality (e.g., fear or danger). It is widely exploited for these qualities in various styles of scary movies and others.

In counterpoint, whether an interval is consonant or dissonant, and how these different qualities are required to be used, is at the heart of the approach to counterpoint.

CHAPTER 2: MELODIC MOTION

Melodic motion refers to the relationship between two melodic lines and which direction they are moving; up, down, or staying the same.

- **Similar** – Two lines move in the same direction, but not the same exact distance. In the following example, we see the top voice moving up a major 3rd, while the bottom voice is also moving up, but spanning a perfect 4th.

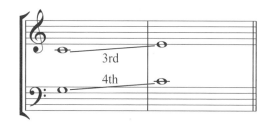

- **Parallel** – For two lines to travel in parallel fashion, they both have to be moving in the same direction as well as the same distance. This means that if one voice was going up a 3rd, the other voice must also be going up a 3rd. If one were moving up a 3rd and the other was moving up a 4th, the motion would be similar, not parallel. (Note: we will not be concerned with interval quality in determining if something is parallel.)

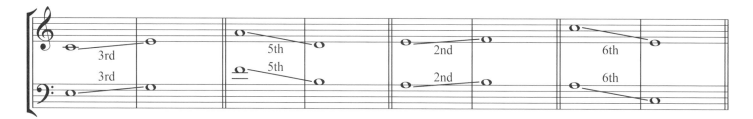

- **Contrary** – Motion where one voice moves in the opposite direction as the other. It does not matter how far in either direction the voices are moving. As long as one is moving up, while the other is moving down, it is in contrary motion.

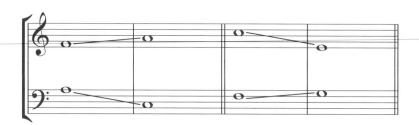

- **Oblique** – One line moves either up or down while the other stays on the same pitch.

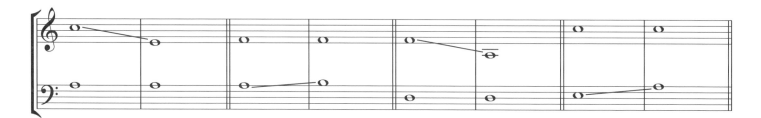

While these examples show one note moving to another single note, descriptions of melodic motion can apply to multiple notes.

Much of what we do when writing counterpoint deals with creating melodic lines, with each having its own identity. When one line is doing something in a bar, we try to have the other line doing something different, but not necessarily all the time. Melodic motion becomes important with this goal. When one line is moving up, it is effective to have the other line moving down, or at least staying the same.

CHAPTER 3: MODES

Traditional species counterpoint makes use of the *church modes*. However, you can still write species counterpoint using the two tonal music modes, better known as the major and minor scales. Since this book will demonstrate the principles of species counterpoint using the modes, the following is a brief explanation as to what exactly the modes are.

The terms "mode" and "scale" are nearly synonymous. The major and natural minor scale are two of the seven church modes. If you take the pitches of a major scale (C, D, E, F, G, A, B, C), and re-order them to start on D (D, E, F, G, A, B, C, D) the placement of the half steps change, from between the 2nd and 3rd scale degrees to between the 6th and 7th scale degrees. The scale beginning on D has a different sound to it because the half steps are in different spots when compared to the C major scale.

You can continue, using the same "white key" pitches, and go from E up to E, this will result in a mode that has the two half steps in different spots. If you continue this procedure of using just the white keys, starting with a different pitch each time, the result is seven distinct modes. No two are exactly alike, as each one has two half steps in a different spot. There are names for each of these modes, listed in the following example, using white keys to demonstrate. The example also shows the order of half and whole steps for each mode (W=whole; H=half).

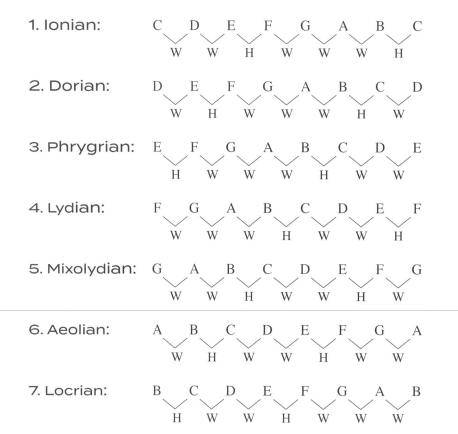

Leaving out Ionian and Aeolian (Ionian mode is the same as the major scale, while Aeolian is the same as the natural minor scale), the five remaining modes can be thought of as sounding similar either to the major scale or the minor scale. For example, the Dorian mode is like the natural minor scale, but with the 6th degree raised a half step. Lydian mode is like the major scale, but with the 4th degree raised a half step. The modes that span a minor 3rd from the 1st to the 3rd degree (Dorian, Phrygian, and Locrian), are similar to the minor scale. The modes which see a major 3rd from the 1st to the 3rd degree (Lydian and Mixolydian) are similar to the major scale.

We will use modes when demonstrating species counterpoint, as it is simpler to deal with just "white key" notes. However, there will also be examples using the notes/scales of different keys instead of the modes. In addition, it is possible to write counterpoint for pitches that do not conform to tonality, those that do not use the major or minor scales, nor the church modes.

CHAPTER 4: MELODY

Counterpoint, at its essence, is about two things: 1. Melody, and 2. The interaction between two or more melodies sounded at the same time. In this section, we will tackle the first element, dealing with melody. To write good counterpoint, one must be able to write a good melody. While two or more different melodies may seem to work well together, in order for the counterpoint to be considered good, each melody must hold up on its own.

DEFINITION

At its most basic level, a *melody* may be defined as an organized linear succession of pitches. "Organized," as opposed to random, means these pitches have a particular contour and rhythm, which work together to form a clear single entity, one that is satisfying in some way. A term such as "pleasing" is problematic, since a melody that is ugly may not be pleasing, but still satisfying, if a certain ugliness is the desired effect in the context of the work as a whole. By "linear" we are referring to one pitch sounded at a time.

MELODY TYPES

There are different types of melodies, all of which fall under this simple definition. A *melodic theme* is perhaps what most people think of as a melody, but motives, riffs, and ostinatos are also considered different types of melodies. The bass line in a rock song can be considered a melody as well. The term "melodic line" might be more appropriate for some of these, in that these melodies are often subordinate or accompanying. In terms of counterpoint, we will cover all different types of melodies, but for now, we will concern ourselves with that of a melodic theme. Such a melody is the primary foreground element in a piece of music, like the main character in a story.

The following example and accompanying audio track have the well-known melodic theme from "Hungarian Dance No. 5" by Johannes Brahms in a rock setting.

MELODIC THEME

 Track 2

Brahms: "Hungarian Dance No.5"

RIFF OR MOTIF

A *riff* is a type of melody that is usually short, and especially in the case of rock and pop music, is repeated multiple times in a row. In classical music, a riff is usually referred to as a "motif" or "motive."

 Track 3

BASS LINE

This is a type of melodic line sounded in the lowest instrument or voice. In rock music, it is often played by the electric bass, but it could be played by any instrument. Bass lines range from playing just the roots or the bottom notes of a chord, to executing more complex lines, akin to riffs or melodic themes. For the purposes of counterpoint, we will be dealing with bass lines that are a bit more complex, those which could exist on their own as interesting melodies or riffs.

 Track 4

OSTINATO

An *ostinato* is similar to a riff, and the terms can be used interchangeably. "Riff" is a popular music term, while "ostinato" is reserved for classical. For a line to be considered an ostinato, the music repeats itself multiple times in a row. Some ostinatos last for entire compositions. Ostinatos are often defined by their rhythmic characteristics, so a pattern which is played on just one pitch could serve as an ostinato. They can be played by any instrument or voice, sounding beneath the other instruments, above, or in the middle. An ostinato sounding in the lowest instrument is also a type of bass line.

 Track 5

In the following rock version of Gustav Holst's "Mars, the Bringer of War," from *The Planets*, the ostinato is rhythmic only.

 Track 6

Holst: "Mars, the Bringer of War" from *The Planets*

CHARACTERISTICS OF A GOOD MELODY

While "good" is subjective, there are certain characteristics that many of the most famous melodies have in common. To many people, a good melody means it is catchy and stays in your head long after you've heard it. To some, a good melody means it is easy to sing. What constitutes a good melody also differs depending on the musical era it belongs to, the style of music in which the melody occurs, as well as whether the melody is vocal or instrumental, and, if instrumental, what instrument is playing the melody. A discussion of all these circumstances might be exhaustive, so the following will cover some of the basic characteristics that help define a good melody.

First off, a melody can be a variety of lengths, from something as short as a few beats (motive), to a complete phrase, or group of several phrases. For now, we will focus on melodies that consist of one or two phrases.

CONTOUR

A good melody has a certain natural contour to it; "natural" as opposed to "mechanical." To use a metaphor, something mechanical might be made up of a repeated pattern, like a staircase, which consists of all right angles, where every step is the same size. Contrast that with the branch of a tree, which follows a variety of directions, at different angles, for different lengths. However, a tree branch may be seen as random, and as stated earlier, a melody is an organized succession of pitches. So, the challenge in creating a good melody is giving the structure a certain organization, while also exhibiting a natural quality. Striking the right balance between these two aesthetics is what constitutes a good melody. There are always exceptions, and some of the most memorable melodies are fairly mechanical.

The following two examples show the same basic melody, but it's obvious that the mechanical version seems more like a pattern, something that may be well suited serving as an accompaniment, but less interesting as a true melodic theme.

 Track 7

Mechanical

 Track 8

Natural

Distance, direction, and rhythm all work together to give a melody a particular contour. In terms of distance, we are referring to melodic intervals. In most good melodies, stepwise motion (melodic 2nds) outnumbers leaps (intervals of a 3rd or larger) to a great degree. While there is no precise recipe for how many steps versus leaps produces the best results, a composer might create a melody that consists of mostly steps, and the leaps are placed carefully and strategically.

 Track 9

Beethoven: "Ecossaise in G"

Notice that in this Beethoven melody, there are never two leaps in a row. When including leaps, it is best to place the leap after a step, then follow the leap with another step. In addition, following a leap with a step that moves in the opposite direction is preferred. Two leaps in a row might be acceptable, but try to avoid more than two. An exception might be when the melody outlines the tones of a chord, sounding root–3rd–5th. But even when arpeggiating a chord, keep this to a minimum. The more the melody keeps arpeggiating a chord, the more it starts to sound like an accompaniment pattern rather than a melody. However, outlining the notes of a chord just enough can provide a proper amount of organization, keeping the melody from sounding random.

Clementi: "Sonatina"

While the first two bars of this melody consist only of leaps, the notes outline that of a C major chord. Also, the stepwise eighth notes beginning in bar 3 help bring contrast, keeping the melody from sounding like an accompaniment pattern.

In terms of "direction," a composer can follow similar guidelines as described with respect to the concept of distance. It is best to avoid traveling for too long in the same direction. In addition, it may be beneficial to vary exactly when the melody switches direction. For example, if the melody moves up for three notes, follow it by traveling down for two. Refrain from starting a regular pattern, where the line moves up for three notes, then down for two, then back up for three, then down for two, etc. However, if such a pattern of directional changes were to take place, one can alleviate the sense of a mechanical pattern by varying the rhythm. Example A shows a melodic line, that changes direction after every four eighth notes. Example B shows all the same pitches in the same order, but the rhythm has been changed to take away some of the mechanical characteristic.

 Track 11

Example A

 Track 12

Example B

4

You may also have noticed that Example A is four measures long, while the less mechanical Example B consists of seven measures. If it was your goal to keep the new, less mechanical melody the same length, this would also be easily achievable.

REPETITION

One major way composers organize sound – whether in creating a melody or thinking about the concept of writing a piece of music as a whole – is to employ repetition. Music relies on some type of repetition to keep it from being perceived as random. In the previous examples (A and B), Example B was characterized by varied rhythms, and repetition was employed in that the melody travels up for four notes, then down for three notes, then up for four, etc. Also note that there is some repetition in rhythm and intervals, where measures 1 and 5 consist of the same rhythm, and the interval between the first two notes in every measure is always a 3rd.

CLIMAX TONE

Many good melodies have a *climax tone* (CT), which is the highest pitch in the melody. For this pitch to be considered a climax tone, there can be only one instance of it. In the following example from Robert Schumann, the high F in the second complete measure serves as the climax tone.

🔊 **Track 13**

Schumann: "The Wild Horseman"

It can help bring out the climactic nature of this tone if the pitch is stressed somehow, such as occurring on a strong beat, perhaps with an accent, or being a longer note. In addition, the climax tone is often most effective when it occurs somewhere a bit off center, occurring near the middle of the melody. Many melodies will start low, gradually ascend to the climax tone, then descend a bit until the end. These are not hard and fast rules. If you are attempting to create a melody and it's not turning out quite right, you can turn to these guidelines and reshape your melody accordingly. Take note of the climax tones in the following melodies from famous composers. Remember, especially when starting out, you can always use your favorite melodies as models.

🔊 **Track 14**

F. Chopin: "Mazurka" (Op. 67 No. 2)

🔊 **Track 15**

Haydn: "Scherzo" from Fourth Sonatina

🔊 **Track 16**

Mozart: "Adagio"

Look at some of your favorite melodies from classical music as well as rock, pop, jazz, showtunes, movie themes, etc. These can be instrumental or vocal melodies. You might find that most, if not all, have a climax tone. Then, make note of where in the melody the climax tone occurs.

CREATING A MELODY

When we look at *species counterpoint* (a kind of exercise governed by a set of rules, where we write a melody against a given melody), we will be dealing with a pre-existing, simple and fixed melody called a *cantus firmus*. However, in exploring real music, making use of concepts within species counterpoint, it will be important to be able to compose real melodies, as opposed to simple exercises. A composer must strike a balance between creating interesting stand-alone melodies and making sure these melodies work when sounded together. It is possible to create two melodies that sound good together as a whole, but traditional counterpoint is also about making sure each melody is interesting when sounded by itself.

When writing counterpoint, it is common to first create one melody, then create a second melody to be played against it. In doing so, we will refer to the first line as the melody, and the second melody will be called the countermelody. This implies that one melody is more important than the other, that one exists as the main melody, and the countermelody accompanies it. However, if the goal is to make both melodies interesting by themselves, the listener may not be able to tell which melody is the main melody and which is the countermelody, depending on how the melodies are used within the structure of the composition. In this case, only the composer really knows that one melody was created first, and the other was created to serve the first melody.

It is also possible to create both (or more than two) melodies simultaneously. Thus, the composer would be working on counterpoint *while* creating the melodies, and the procedure of contrapuntal writing gives birth to the melodies. Either method works in creating counterpoint. For now, we will focus on first creating one good melodic theme, (where "theme" is used to describe a melody that holds some significance within a composition).

REFINED IMPROVISATION

We already covered some characteristics that comprise a good melody. Now, we will demonstrate one method for creating a melody. There are many ways to go about this task. Some people improvise on an instrument, often piano or guitar, but it could be any instrument. The improvisation eventually yields an appealing melody. Then the composer refines the melody, taking the raw, improvised material, and enhancing it.

When your improvising produces something with which you are happy, you can then refine it, according to the characteristics of a good melody previously discussed. Let's say the following came out of some improvisation.

 **Track 17**

Having the melody notated allows a composer to easily examine the melody, as it is, frozen in time. You may notice that the improvised melody does not have a climax tone. The highest note in the melody is a G, but there are two of them. There are at least a few options to remedy this imperfection. We could take one of those Gs and raise it, making it the single highest note. Or we could take the first G and lower it to some other pitch. Another option would be to take the note that immediately follows the second G and raise it. It is, after all, a longer note, which is often good in a climax tone. The following example does just that. However, this change seemed to make what comes right after it a bit awkward. So, instead of an E on beat 1 of the third bar, it has been changed to an A.

 Track 18

Although it isn't a necessary part of counterpoint, you may wish to think about chords that harmonize the melody. Your composition, especially if it's a rock or pop tune, might make use of chords for most of the tune. Thinking about what chords might accompany a melody can also help shape the melody in a way that improves upon it. For example, if this melody were in the key of A minor, you might be aware that the V or "dominant" chord in this key is an E major chord. This harmony is seen as unstable and is good for creating a kind of question mark on the first phrase of a two-phrase melody. Looking at the climax tone, B is part of an E major chord, and thus works well as a pitch on which to end the first phrase. This helps make the phrase a question, and then the second phrase can exist as an answer. Next, we can consider the very last note. Since the melody probably would end on the *tonic* chord of A minor, ending the melody on an A would be the most conclusive sounding. Ending on a C is part of an A minor chord, but it might be better if we end on an A instead.

Track 19

Simply changing the final C to an A caused the last few notes to sound a bit awkward, so the two notes before the final note were changed to B and G♯, which outline the dominant (E) chord. At the end of a phrase, going from the dominant chord to the tonic chord is known as an *authentic cadence*. A cadence is the progression of two different chords at the end of a phrase, which give it a musical punctuation. An authentic cadence is one which promotes a conclusive end. There will be further discussion regarding counterpoint and chord progressions in Chapter Six.

After this step, we can examine the contour and rhythm of the melody. Does it have a natural shape to it? Does anything about it seem mechanical? Our original melody had a bit of a *sequence* (a short melodic figure that gets repeated, but at a different transposition level) to it, where beginning in the penultimate bar, beat 4, we have eighth notes that rise by a step, then descend by a 3rd. Some of the changes we made to the melody already broke up this sequence a bit. It should also be noted that a sequence is not necessarily a bad thing. They often happen in the accompaniment, or in spots other than a main melody. Even in a main theme, a sequence can work just fine. It depends on the context, as well as how long it lasts. Knowing that, having a sequence in a melody may detract from a more natural shape. If you find your melody is not quite working for you, or you at least feel it can be better, try removing the sequence, something we already did to our melody in its current stage.

With respect to rhythm, our melody is simple, dominated by quarter and eighth notes. This simplicity makes it sound mechanical, but perhaps it works for you. You may try to enhance the rhythm, but then find it is best in this simpler incarnation. For the purposes of this book, we will attempt to make it a little more expressive with some rhythmic enhancements. Before attempting this, it is important to note that we haven't mentioned the tempo of this melody, (aside from hearing the tempo on the accompanying audio tracks). Perhaps you don't know the tempo and have been assuming some middle-of-the-road pace of the music. As you work on composing other parts, if you realize the tempo is going to be significantly different from what you initially thought, you can make rhythmic adjustments. We will be working at a tempo of ♩ = 100. Examine the rhythmic alterations in the next example. There are endless possibilities. However, keeping the half notes in place at the ends of each of the two phrases is something that helped the structure of the melody, showing the clear punctuation at these division points.

Track 20

♩ = 100

Now that the melody is less mechanical, compare this version with the first version. You may be happy with something you created, whether it be a melody, chord progression, or an accompaniment pattern such as an ostinato. But take the time to examine your creation and think about making it better. Knowing some compositional techniques – such as the characteristics of a good melody, or how to harmonize a melody with chords so that it exists as a clear phrase, with a solid cadence – allows you to examine your creation and employ the techniques you've learned.

Doing so may make it better. But sometimes, any changes you make produces something that is not quite as good, so you end up satisfied with what you have.

MELODY FROM CHORD PROGRESSIONS

A composer must be able to generate material using creativity to form interesting musical ideas. Some refer to inspiration – such as a painting a composer studied – as setting off the musical creative process and helping generate ideas. To others, certain impactful life events may drive the composer to create music in certain ways. Often, the main melodic themes of a piece of music are the most important element. They are like the main characters in a story. So, it may seem logical that a composer first works to try to create one or more strong melodic themes, and then everything else which makes up the composition, is created to serve and support these themes. But there are different ways to create a melody. Some composers prefer to create an interesting chord progression, perhaps one that is characterized by specific rhythms, which the composer feels enhance the progression in positive ways. Then, playing this chord progression, and listening carefully, the composer creates a melody which is born from this chord progression. For some, hearing a series of chords makes melodies jump out at them.

The following example shows a chord progression in the key of C minor, with some rhythmic interest to it.

Track 21

The composer can play this progression, and perhaps hear a melody rise out of it. Or, the composer can improvise along with the chord progression, and that will give birth to interesting melodies. The next example shows a melody which was created from the previous chord progression. Note in measure 2, the Bdim followed by the G major chord. If we combine the notes of both chords, it forms a G7 (G-B-D-F). The G in the melody on the "and" of beat 2 – even though that pitch does not belong to a Bdim chord – was chosen to turn the Bdim chord into a G7, the full dominant seventh chord of the key (C minor).

Track 22

It is important to realize that the chord progression was used to help get the creative engine going, to help create a melody. However, this does not mean that the chord progression must be used in the composition. It could be that it just served the purpose of helping create a melody. But in the actual composition, this melody will be accompanied by other melodies, whether counter melodies in an inner voice, or a bass line. Or perhaps different chords are used to harmonize the melody.

It should also be mentioned that a melody is more than just pitches and rhythm at a certain tempo. Dynamics, articulation, and other expressive elements, as well as what instrument(s) will be playing the melody are important factors.

MELODY FROM "SCRATCH"

This refers to creating a melody in some other way than improvising or from an existing chord progression. One method is to compose a melody, one note at a time, perhaps constructing it through the process of inputing it in a notation software, and then playing it back. Each time you hear it, you add more onto it or change it in some way.

Another method might simply involve hearing it in your head. It does not come from improvising; rather, the sounds just form in your head, perhaps while doing something special such as hiking, going to a museum, or watching a movie. The composer must then find a way to get this melody from their head to realization. This means either notating it or recording it. Once that is done, the composer can then tweak the melody, enhancing it using methods previously discussed.

Composers rarely stick exclusively to one method, no matter how reliable it may be. You are encouraged to experiment. With respect to counterpoint, the important thing is that having good melodies is at the foundation of this compositional technique.

PART TWO:
SPECIES COUNTERPOINT – PRINCIPLES

TWO-VOICE COUNTERPOINT

This chapter deals with a traditional set of counterpoint principles, established in 1725. If you're a rock 'n' roll composer, you might be doubting the relevance of music from almost 300 years ago. However, these contrapuntal principles are prevalent in a wide variety of music today, including many forms of popular music. Rock/pop song-writers, who are composing from the gut, based on feel, are often using these rules without knowing it. They are what guide a composer into creating something that simply sounds good. If a composer has a clear understanding of these rules, they can still compose based on feel, but in cases where something just isn't sounding quite right, instead of blindly and endlessly tweaking the music until they find something they like, they can turn to the rules and get much faster results. Besides achieving results more quickly, the music has a better chance of sounding as good as possible, instead of simply acceptable.

The intervals between two voices will be described in terms of an octave or smaller, known as *simple intervals*. Occasionally, *compound intervals* will be used. These are intervals greater than an octave, such as a 10th, which is an octave plus a 3rd. However, in most cases, compound intervals will be labeled as simple intervals (i.e., using "3rd" instead of "10th"). This is done in part because the rules regarding a 10th are the same as those of a 3rd, and it is easier to write the simple interval.

VOICE LEADING

Before we delve into species counterpoint, there is one concept that applies to all linear writing: *voice leading*. We refer to the individual melodic lines as voices, and it is these voices that interact to create harmony. Voice leading is how each line progresses, from one note to the next, in consideration with how it interacts with the other line or lines. In counterpoint, we focus more on the individual voices, and how they interact (the intervals produced at each point where notes are sounded at the same time) and are not as concerned with what harmony (chords) might be resulting. Counterpoint is a different type of writing, referred to as *polyphony* (as opposed to homophony, where one melodic line gets harmonized by chords). With voice leading, where a line is going is just as important as where the line has been. In other words, the context of any single note in a melody is important. A quarter note sounded at the same time as two eighth notes may sound fine in isolation. However, we must consider what came right before the note and what is coming after, to make sure the note at hand is the best choice.

SPECIES COUNTERPOINT

If you play an instrument, you've probably learned to play scales. Scales are a way for your fingers to learn to play in different keys. Becoming a skilled improvisor often relies on having scales memorized, where they can be comfortably executed in one's fingers. They may also serve as exercises to warm up the fingers and work on strength and dexterity. Species counterpoint is an exercise for similar purposes, a warm-up for composers, but more intellectual. Many years ago, a composer might write one or more species counterpoint exercises before starting work on composing a piece of music. Since species counterpoint deals with a specific set of rules designed to produce the most appropriate and desired sounds between two melodic lines, a composer may wish to make an understanding and implementation of these rules second nature. Just like a player doesn't want to have to think carefully about playing the correct notes in a scale, rather execute them fluently without thought, a composer may wish the same when it comes to creating two simultaneous melodies. A composer who engages in species counterpoint as a regular warm up will eventually develop great skill in writing effective counterpoint, without having to labor on it exhaustively.

After learning the rules of species counterpoint, you are encouraged to engage in these exercises on a regular basis. But because this is music, don't just write. Make sure to play and/or sing every exercise, to fully hear and understand what you are doing and why these rules are in place.

This system of counterpoint is perhaps first and best illustrated in a theoretical text written by Johann Joseph Fux in 1725, titled *Gradus ad Parnassum*. It is an approach to counterpoint where we create a melodic line in counterpoint to a given melody called the *cantus firmus*. Species counterpoint attempts to focus on the intervals between notes in the cantus firmus and the countermelody being created. It does this by taking the element of rhythm mostly out of the equation and focuses on the intervals. Species counterpoint is sometimes referred to as "strict counterpoint," with origins in the 18th century. Even though these rules might seem restricting to the modern composer, they have their value, serving as a foundation on which to build upon. A composer can start out using species counterpoint rules as a guide, then break free of them when it serves their greater vision when something isn't working, the rules of species counterpoint can also be drawn upon when creating two melodic lines in counterpoint. Sometimes going back and reshaping something to conform to traditional rules provides the solution for which you're seeking.

After a presentation of the principles of species counterpoint, you will have a chance to see how these principles can be applied to real music. Because working with species counterpoint is an exercise, to keep it simple, the cantus firmus will consist of only whole notes. The counterpoint line to be written against the cantus firmus will also exist in simple rhythms. The different species reflect how many notes there are in the counterpoint for every single note in the cantus firmus, or in the case of fourth species, a particular type of suspended dissonance in the counterpoint for every single note in the cantus firmus. (If this doesn't make sense right now, don't worry it will be explained shortly). When adapting a species counterpoint exercise into real music, rhythms are changed to turn the exercise into something musical. However, keep in mind that when a composer wishes to write counterpoint in a piece of real music, starting with a species counterpoint exercise is not necessarily the way to do it. Species exercises are just that, exercises. A composer doesn't first write a scale, and then attempt to alter that scale into a piece of music.

CANTUS FIRMUS

The *cantus firmus* (CF) is a fixed melody representing one phrase of music. It is fixed in that in the practice of writing counterpoint, this melody cannot be changed. When you write counterpoint for your own compositions, even if you have a main melody you've created, and you're attempting to compose a countermelody to be sounded against it, you have the freedom to change your original melody to better serve your composition. For the purposes of species writing, the cantus firmus cannot be changed.

THE COUNTERPOINT

The *counterpoint* (CP) refers to the second voice, the one you will be creating to accompany the cantus firmus. For each note in the cantus firmus, there will be one or more notes in the counterpoint, depending on which species is being practiced.

CHAPTER 5: FIRST SPECIES COUNTERPOINT – 1:1

In *first species*, there will be one note in the counterpoint for each note in the cantus firmus. First species is sometimes represented as 1:1 or one against one. There are a few simple rules to follow when writing first species. It is important to follow the steps in a specific order to achieve the best results. Instead of starting at the beginning and writing one note at a time until we get to the end of the line, we start the counterpoint by writing the first measure, then skip to the end and write the last three measures. Also note that in species counterpoint, we generally write in Dorian, Phrygian, Lydian, Mixolydian, Aeolian, or Ionian modes.

The following are two completed first species exercises, taken from Johann Joseph Fux's *Gradus ad Parnassum* (1725). One includes the counterpoint line above the cantus firmus, and the other below the cantus firmus. Notice that the intervals between the two voices have been written between the two staves. This is a handy method to check your work, and it makes the process of observing intervals faster. Also notice that CT is used to label the climax tone. It's a good habit to label this yourself, as it will help make sure you always have a climax tone.

🔊 **Track 23**

Fux: *Gradus ad Parnassum,* First Species with CP Above

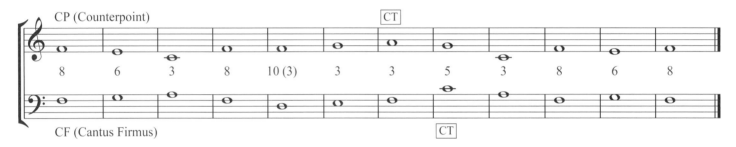

Fux: *Gradus ad Parnassum,* First Species with CP Below

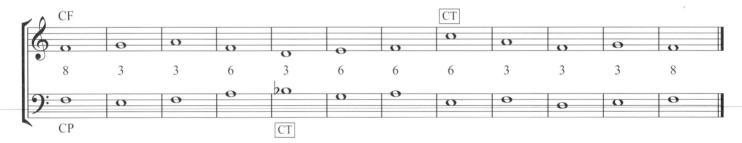

BEGINNING THE COUNTERPOINT

When writing a counterpoint above the cantus firmus, the first note should be a perfect (P) 1, P5, or P8.

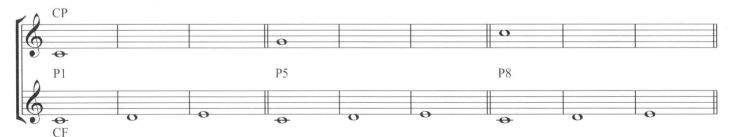

When writing a counterpoint below the cantus firmus, the first note should be a P1 or a P8.

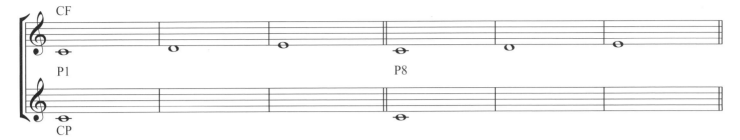

ENDING THE COUNTERPOINT

When utilizing the modes mentioned earlier, the CF will end by stepping down to the *tonic* (the note that names the mode, e.g., in D Dorian, a D). So, in C Ionian, the CF will always end on a C, preceded by a D. The interval between the last note in both lines will be either an octave or unison. The CP will end differently, depending on the mode being used. Notice that the penultimate note in the counterpoint will always be a leading tone; in other words, a half step below the final note. This means that in Dorian, Mixolydian, and Aeolian, the penultimate note must be raised a half step. For each mode, there is a standard way to end the counterpoint, so it is beneficial to memorize these endings.

🔊 **Track 24**

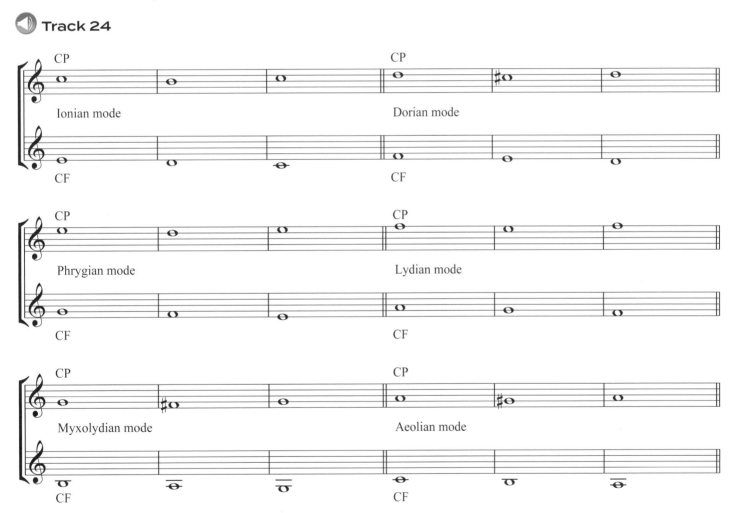

As seen in the previous example, in Aeolian mode, the G must be turned into G♯. An important rule to follow is to put at least two measures in between a G♯ and G, should you have another G in your counterpoint. The sound of a G too close to a G♯ would sound chromatic, or as if we have an altered note outside the key. Putting some distance between the G and G♯ does not produce this altered sound. This is a rule of traditional species counterpoint. However, if you are composing a rock tune, breaking this rule may be just fine as the chromatic sound is desirable to you.

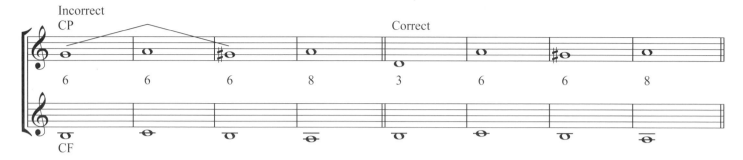

WRITING THE REMAINING NOTES

Remember that while one of the goals is to create a countermelody that sounds "good" when played against the first melody, another goal is to make the countermelody sound good by itself as well. In working with species counterpoint, where all rhythmic interest as well as other expressive characteristics are stripped away, one should still strive to create an interesting contour. This means including a climax tone. Remember to always play and/or sing everything you're writing, at every step. This includes playing the CF before you even begin writing any notes for the CP. As you write the beginning and ending of your CP, try to imagine an interesting contour, including where the climax tone might best be placed. While it's not necessary, a good rule to follow is to have your climax tone in the CP occur in a different spot from the climax tone in the CF. In addition, if doing this in pencil, write lightly and be prepared to erase.

Before proceeding to the voice leading rules, take note of the following completed first species counterpoint. See how the individual contour of each line, and that the climax tones are in different spots. Also, while there are plenty of leaps, most only span a 3rd. Larger leaps (i.e., 4ths, 5ths, 6ths) are used seldomly, and should be spaced apart (i.e., after a leap of a fifth, one should not write another large leap only two measures later). More characteristics will be covered following an explanation of the voice leading rules. For now, take note of how different parts of the exercise are labeled. Always mark which line is the CF and which line is the CP. Mark the interval between the two voices. While it is not necessary to include the interval quality, it makes for good practice, to ensure that intervals of a 5th are always perfect (diminished 5ths are not allowed). Remember "CT" stands for climax tone. It may be helpful to label this; that way, you will always remember to include one in your melodic lines.

🔊 **Track 26**

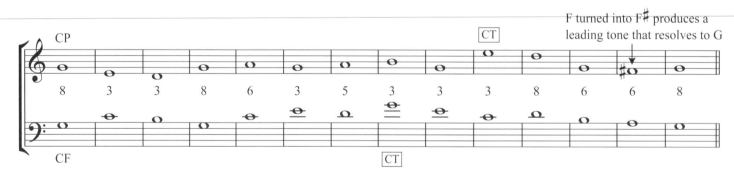

In first species, the only allowable intervals between the two voices are the M3, m3, P5, M6, m6, and P8. The intervals of a 3rd plus an octave (10), 5th plus octave (12) and 6th plus octave (13) are also allowed. These larger intervals should occur when the lines are set further apart. In species counterpoint, an appropriate line should span a smaller range due to the fact that species counterpoint assumes the singing voice as the instrument. However, when dealing with instruments as well as "real music," especially modern popular music, one does not need to restrict the melodic line to such a narrow range. For now, in examining species counterpoint, we will adhere to these stricter guidelines.

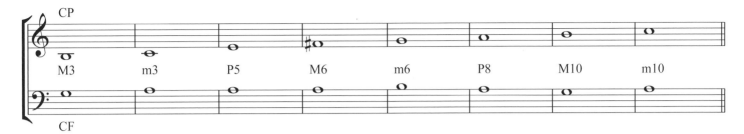

Besides the allowable intervals between voices, there are basic principles for voice leading; in other words, the context of these intervals. These principles are based on types of melodic motion. (See Chapter Two.)

1. From one perfect consonance to another perfect consonance, use contrary or oblique motion. **Note:** a P4 is not considered a perfect consonance in species counterpoint, because it sounds unstable or unresolved compared to the P5 or octave.

Track 28

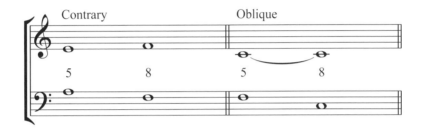

2. From a perfect consonance to an imperfect consonance (e.g., 3rd or 6th), use similar, contrary, or oblique motion.

Track 29

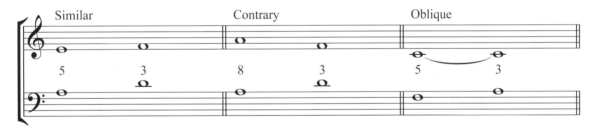

3. From an imperfect consonance to a perfect consonance, use contrary or oblique motion.

Track 30

4. From an imperfect consonance to another imperfect consonance, use contrary, similar, parallel, or oblique motion.

Track 31

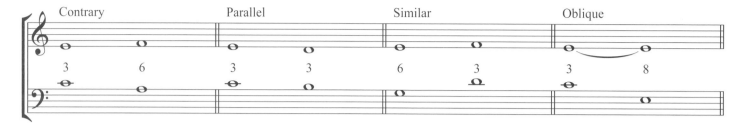

In addition to the four basic principles of voice leading, consider the following rules.

- Do not include more than two tied notes. This means oblique motion will be used sparingly, if at all. If working with a particularly long melodic line, two ties might be desirable, but try to put some distance between them.

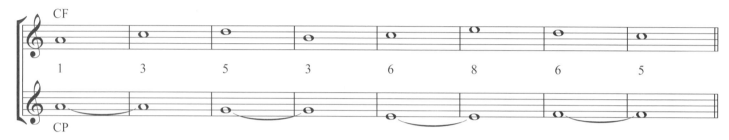

- Avoid too much parallel motion, breaking it up with at least one spot of oblique or contrary motion. Remember that only 3rds and 6ths are allowed for parallel motion, and too much of it destroys the independence between each melodic line and starts to sound mechanical.

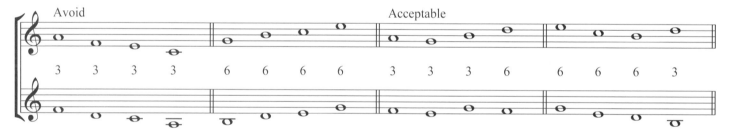

Earlier, we looked at a completed exercise where the CP was in the top voice. Study the next example, which sees the CP in the bottom voice. Also note the ending, where the CF steps down to the tonic, while the CP plays a leading tone, resolving upwards, just as when the CP was on the top.

Track 32

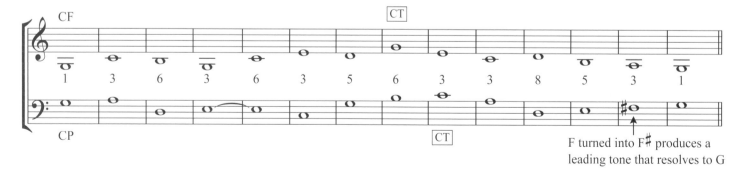

F turned into F♯ produces a
leading tone that resolves to G

The following are two different cantus firmi for you to practice your first species writing. For each CF, write a CP below, and then one above. However, feel free to write even more, and use your ears to help judge which ones are best. You may rewrite the CF in a different octave on staff paper if you like. Remember to write in the clef, as is good practice. Play/listen to what you are doing through each step of the process. Start out by playing and/or singing the CF multiple times. If using an electronic keyboard with different instrument patches, be aware that sounds with considerable sustain are best (i.e., violin, flute, trumpet, etc.). Piano and guitar are okay for this purpose.

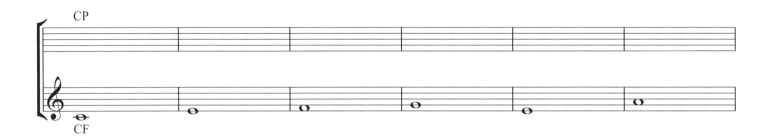

CHAPTER SUMMARY

- One note in counterpoint for each note in cantus firmus

- First measure:
  - First note above a cantus firmus is a P1, P5, or P8
  - First note below a cantus firmus is a P1 or P8

- Ending:
  - Always end with the CF stepping down to the tonic and a P1 or P8 between the two lines

- Writing:
  - Allowable intervals M3, m3, P5, M6, m6, and P8
  - P4 is not considered a consonance and cannot be used
  - From a perfect consonance to another perfect consonance, use contrary or oblique motion
  - From a perfect consonance to an imperfect consonance, use similar, contrary, or oblique motion
  - From an imperfect consonance to a perfect consonance, use contrary or oblique motion
  - From an imperfect consonance to another imperfect consonance, use contrary, similar, parallel, or oblique motion

CHAPTER 6: SECOND SPECIES COUNTERPOINT – 2:1

In second species counterpoint there are two notes for each note in the CF. Basic principles from first species and writing a melody still apply.

The following are two completed second species exercises taken from Johann Joseph Fux's *Gradus ad Parnassum* (1725). One includes the counterpoint line above the cantus firmus, and the other, below. Dissonant intervals (m2, M2, P4, d5, m7 M7) are also circled. More will be explained about this a bit later. Also notice that the final note is a D, meaning this is written in dorian mode. In measure 3, we use a C natural – which is characteristic of that mode. In the penultimate measure, we use a C♯, making it a leading tone that resolves to the tonic (D).

 **Track 33**

Fux: *Gradus ad Parnassum,* Second Species with CP AEove

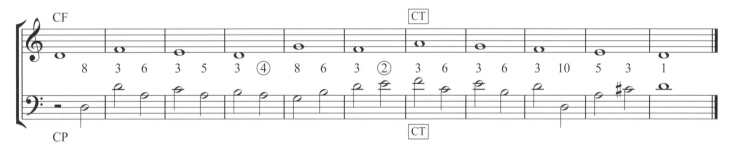

Fux: *Gradus ad Parnassum,* Second Species with CP Below

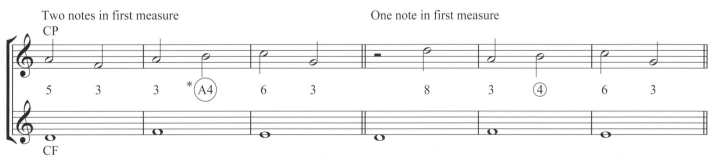

BEGINNING THE COUNTERPOINT

In the first measure, the CP may contain either two half notes, or a half rest followed by a half note.

 **Track 34**

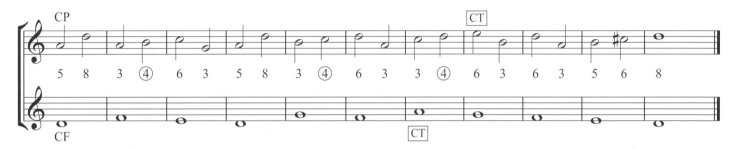

* In m. 2 of the first example, the 4th is an augmented 4th. Since both the perfect and augmented 4ths are considered dissonant, it is not necessary to label it as an "A4." However, you may find it useful as a way to check what your ears are perceiving.

The first note of the CP must form a perfect consonance (P1, P8, or P5, not P4) with the CF.

ENDING THE COUNTERPOINT

You may end the CP with two half notes in the penultimate measure, or a whole note. Whichever note is the penultimate, it must be a *leading tone* (a half step beneath the final note), whether you are writing the CP above or below the CF.

 **Track 35**

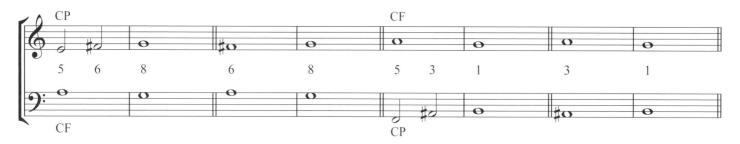

WRITING THE REMAINING NOTES

There are six basic principles for voice leading in second species.

1. The first half note in each measure must be a consonance (either perfect or imperfect). This is just like first species, in that beat 1 of each measure features a consonance.

2. The second half of the measure is where we get to create some dissonance, a phenomenon that helps propel the music forward. However, it is not required that a dissonance occurs here, only that it may. If using a dissonance, it must be a particular type known as a *passing tone* (PT). A PT is characterized by an approach by step and then resolved by step in the same direction. In other words, you cannot leap to or from a dissonance. The allowable dissonances are M2, m2, P4, A4 (A = augmented), d5 (d = diminished), M7, and m7.

 **Track 36**

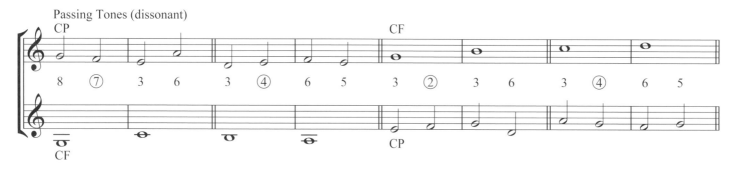

Note that in the exercise, when labeling the intervals, dissonances are circled. Follow this practice when you write and label your own counterpoint exercises.

3. If two measures in a row have the same perfect consonance on beat 1, the perceived effect is that the note in between them (the note in the second half of the measure) is not present. In other words, it will sound as if there is a parallel octave or 5th, something that is not allowed.

Track 37

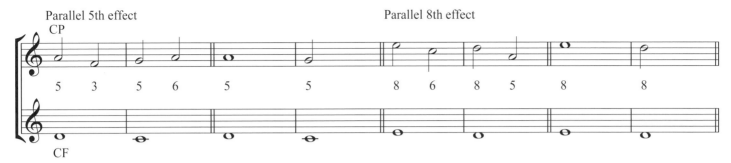

4. A unison is acceptable in the second half of the measure, but never on beat 1.

Track 38

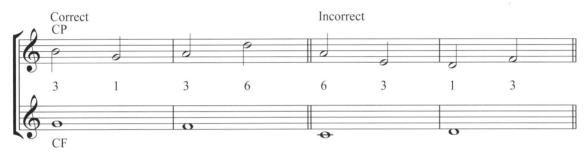

5. Approach and depart from leaps greater than a 3rd in contrary motion, traveling by step. This is not a hard and fast rule, rather something that will give you the best results a majority of the time. If you chose not to follow this recommendation in any instance, make sure the result sounds good to you. It may mean that failing to use contrary motion after the larger leap ends up giving you a better melody, better counterpoint between the two melodies, or both.

Track 39

6. Repeated notes, tied notes, and sequences (an interval pattern that repeats itself multiple times, but at different transposition levels) are not allowed. Also unacceptable are repeated melodic figures that can sound mechanical, destroying the organic nature that characterized a good melody.

Track 40

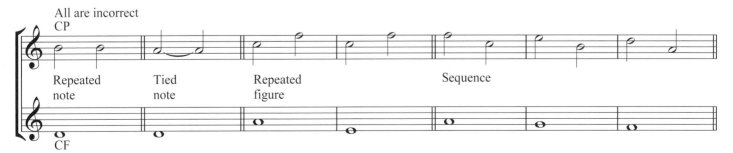

It should be noted that elements that can sound mechanical – characteristics that may ruin the organic nature of a melody – are principles of strict counterpoint. Being mechanical may be acceptable in alternative music styles such as rock/pop or film music, which borrows from multiple different styles. Breaking such rules or just not following recommended principles may result in something that does not sound good to you. Or, perhaps it does sound good; then, at its worst it may sound stylistically inappropriate. This means, if you were scoring a film set in the late 18th century and you wanted some authentic sounding classical music of the era, you might be able to capture this style superficially. Strictly following rules such as these principles of traditional counterpoint will help in the authenticity.

The following are two different cantus firmi for you to practice your second species writing. For each CF, write a CP above, and then one below the CF.

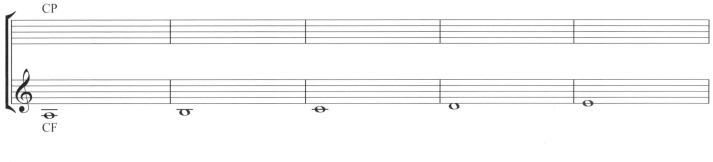

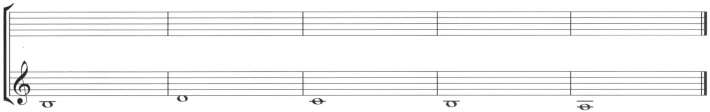

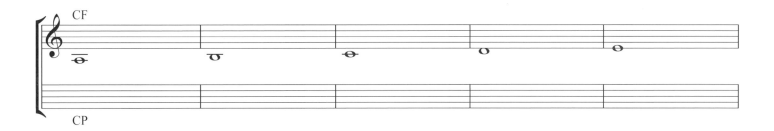

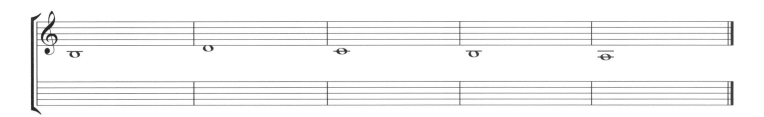

CHAPTER SUMMARY

- Two notes in counterpoint for each note in cantus firmus

- First measure:
    - CP begins with a half note or half rest followed by a half note
    - First note must be a perfect consonance

- Ending:
    - Penultimate measure ends with a whole note or two half notes
    - Penultimate note must be a leading tone

- Writing:
    - First half note must be a consonance
    - Dissonance must be a passing tone
    - Do not place the same perfect consonance on beat 1, two bars in a row
    - Unisons are acceptable in the second half of the measure, never on beat 1
    - Approach and depart leaps greater than a 3rd in contrary motion
    - Repeated notes, tied notes, and sequences are not allowed

CHAPTER 7: THIRD SPECIES COUNTERPOINT – 4:1

Third species sees four notes in the CP for every note in the CF. There is no species featuring 3:1, because strict counterpoint does not make use of triplets.

The following are two completed third species exercises, taken from Johann Joseph Fux's *Gradus ad Parnassum* (1725). One includes the counterpoint line above the cantus firmus, and the other, below.

🔊 **Track 41**

Fux: *Gradus ad Parnassum,* Third Species with CP Above

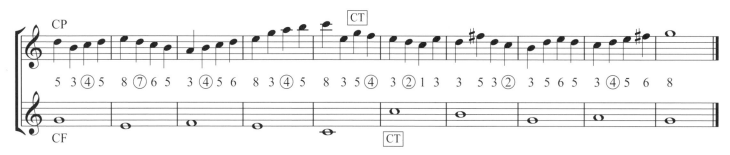

Fux: *Gradus ad Parnassum,* Third Species with CP Below

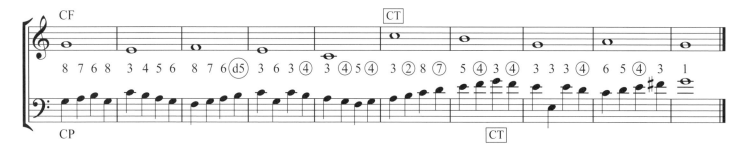

BEGINNING THE COUNTERPOINT

The first measure of the CP may begin with either a quarter note or a quarter rest. Also, the first note in the CP must form a perfect consonance with the CF (whether the CP begins with a quarter note or a quarter rest). In addition, the allowable consonances for the first notes are the same first and second species counterpoint.

 **Track 42**

ENDING THE COUNTERPOINT

Just as first and second species, the second-to-last note in the CP must be a leading tone. The following are some commonly used patterns for the ending of a third species counterpoint exercise. However, these are not the only possible endings, and you are free to come up with one of your own.

🔊 **Track 43**

(Note: Here is a situation where the F♮ is acceptable, because there are two notes in between this and the F♯ leading tone.)

Note that, in the second example, beat 2, there is a dissonance from which the departure is not a step. There are other types of dissonances, besides the PT allowed in third species. More on that, shortly.

WRITING THE REMAINING NOTES

There are six basic principles for voice leading in second species.

1. The first note in each measure must be a consonance. You should realize by now that this principle applies throughout species counterpoint. So, even when you're composing popular music, this is a good rule to follow.

2. The remaining three notes may be dissonant or consonant, but one of the last two notes should be a consonance. This means the only place where two dissonances in a row are allowed is on beats 2 and 3.

🔊 **Track 44**

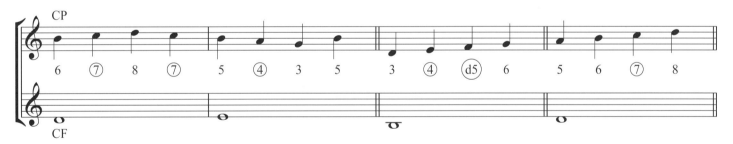

3. If you choose any dissonances for the measure, the following are allowed: passing tone (both accented and unaccented), neighbor tone (NT), and nota cambiata (NC). The latter is the only dissonance that features a leap away from the dissonant interval.

🔊 **Track 45**

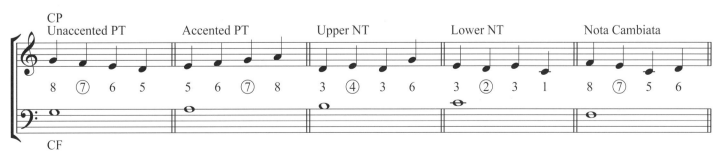

For passing tones, accented means to be on beats 1 or 3. Unaccented is a note that occurs on beats 2 or 4.

Neighbor tones see the same pitch both before and after the dissonance. You can further describe NTs as "upper" or "lower."

The *nota cambiata* always has the same interval pattern: a step down to the dissonance, a 3rd down (away from the dissonance), then a step up. The first and third notes in this pattern must be consonant, but the second and fourth notes may be dissonant.

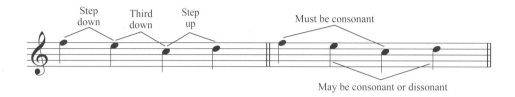

The nota cambiata does not have to begin on beat 1, but can also begin on beat 3, meaning it can traverse two measures.

🔊 **Track 46**

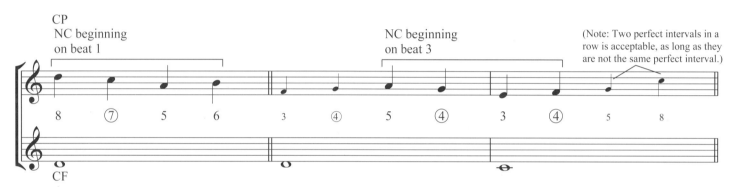

It's interesting to note that in the Renaissance period (16th and early 17th centuries) where the NC primarily occurred, leaping away from a dissonance was considered inappropriate. To our modern ears, a violation of this rule may not sound like there's anything wrong with it. Yet, it was determined back then that a leap away from a dissonance sounded okay in a particular set of circumstances.

4. When you have perfect consonances such as P5ths or P8ths, allow at least two notes in between them. If these perfect intervals are too close together, they can sound like parallel perfect intervals, something uncharacteristic.

🔊 **Track 47**

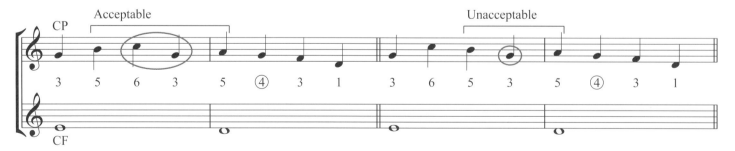

5. Avoid repeated melodic motives, which can start to sound like patterns, something that is undesirable in traditional counterpoint. (Remember, this may be okay for rock/pop or other forms of contemporary music.) Keep your eyes/ears out for any place where four to six notes are repeated (not just the actual pitches, but the same interval pattern). Patterns will be perceived, especially if the motives are close together in the line, as in the following example, which sees only three notes in between the two motives.

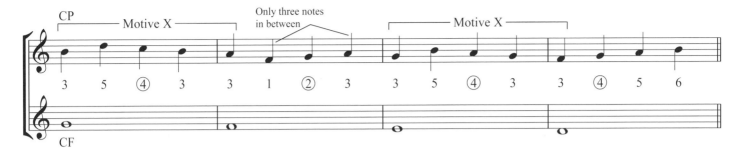

If you put more space in between the motives, the repetition will become less noticeable, and therefore acceptable. There is no rule for exactly how many notes/beats in between motives is acceptable. Use your ears to judge whether you notice it. The following example sees the same motives as in the previous example, but with more distance in between.

Track 49

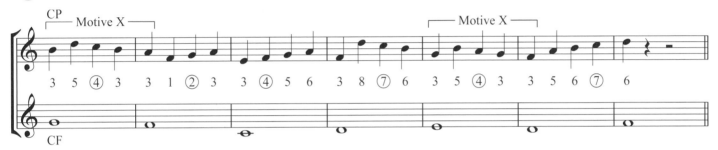

6. Do not write a succession of leaps that form *arpeggios* (broken/melodic chord). This can make your melodic line sound more like an accompaniment pattern than a true melody.

Track 50

When writing counterpoint, remember to use your ears as well as your eyes. You might miss something when just looking at the notation, but a broken rule might jump out at you if listening to it. Anytime you hear something that doesn't sound quite right, it may be that you've broken a rule.

As mentioned before, when writing modern music (pop/rock, or even "contemporary classical"), there are some situations where breaking certain rules or at least going against a recommendation gives you the sound you want. For example, if you are attempting to write a countermelody, if a subordinate or accompaniment role is what you want, then using arpeggio figures is okay. But be careful; breaking too many rules can lead to a composition that's chaotic and lacking direction. If you break a rule, make note of it, and try to break that same rule in the same way multiple times, throughout the composition.

The following are two different cantus firmi for you to practice your third species writing. For each CF, write a CP above and then one below the CF.

CHAPTER SUMMARY

- Four notes in counterpoint for each note in cantus firmus

- First Measure:
  - ❭ Must begin with either a quarter note or quarter rest
  - ❭ Allowable consonances are the same as first and second species counterpoint

- Ending:
  - ❭ Penultimate note must end with a leading tone

- Writing:
  - ❭ First note in each measure must be a consonance
  - ❭ One of the last two notes should be a consonance
  - ❭ Allowable voice leading with dissonant intervals: passing tone, neighbor tone, and nota cambiata
  - ❭ Allow at least two notes in between P5th or P8ths
  - ❭ Avoid repeated melodic motives
  - ❭ If you have two dissonances in a row, make sure they are on beats 2 and 3

CHAPTER 8: FOURTH SPECIES COUNTERPOINT – SYNCOPATED

By "syncopated," we are referring to *suspensions*. A suspension is a dissonance that occurs when a pitch from the previous note or chord hangs on while all the other voices move to a new chord. In the following example, we see an F major chord followed by a C major chord. When the C chord occurs, the F from the previous chord is still sounding, as if that note/voice were daydreaming and didn't realize everyone else had moved on to a new chord. But then the F resolves down to an E, so that it fully belongs to the new chord.

In counterpoint, even though we're not dealing with chords, the same concept applies, with respect to dissonant intervals. In fourth species, we are not only allowed to include dissonances on beat 1, but we are encouraged to do so as often as possible. This dissonance on the downbeat demands a resolution, and the constant tension and release created by this, propels the music forward.

The following are two completed fourth species exercises. One includes the counterpoint line above the cantus firmus, and the other, below. Listen for the dissonances on beat 1, which then resolves, and hear how the "push and pull" sounds satisfying.

🔊 **Track 51**

Fux: *Gradus ad Parnassum,* Fourth Species with CP Above

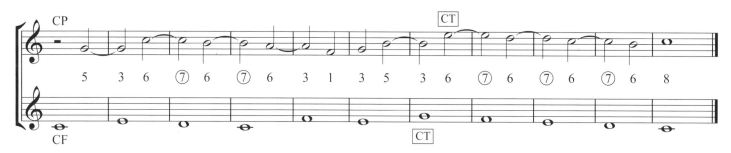

Fux: *Gradus ad Parnassum,* Fourth Species with CP Below

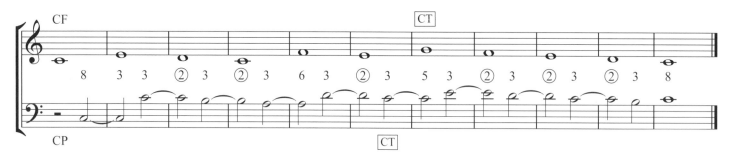

BEGINNING THE COUNTERPOINT

Begin with a half rest followed by a half note. The first note should be one of the allowable consonances from the other species.

🔊 **Track 52**

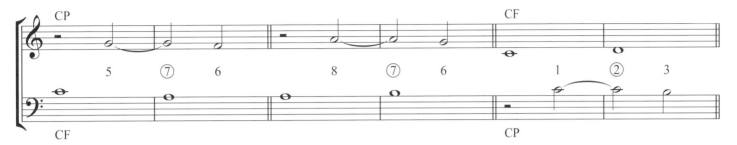

ENDING THE COUNTERPOINT

Just like in other species, the CP must land on the leading tone on the penultimate note. The following are some common patterns in fourth species.

🔊 **Track 53**

WRITING THE REMAINING NOTES

The following principles should be followed in writing the bulk of your CP line. Writing in fourth species requires you to look ahead to see which interval will be created when your tied note is sounded with the note at the beginning of the next measure. Since the inclusion of as many dissonances as possible is the desired effect in this species, you should try to write notes that, when tied to the next measure, will always be dissonant. If you always try for a dissonance, there may be a couple places where the creation of a dissonance is not possible, and thus your exercise will have at least a couple consonances. Then, you'll end up having a completed exercise that is dominated by dissonances, with no more than a few consonances, which can lead to a nice, non-mechanical counterpoint.

1. The second half note in every measure must be a consonance.

2. The first half note in each measure may be consonant or dissonant, but the only dissonance allowed is the suspension. There are three allowable suspension patterns, labeled by the dissonant interval followed by the consonant interval: 7–6, 4–3, and 2–3.

🔊 **Track 54**

3. First, try for a dissonance/suspension when you write each measure. If it does not work out, write tied consonant notes. Remember, the intervals created between the two lines are not the only priority in writing counterpoint. The other priority is creating a new line that holds up on its own as a strong melody. Even though you might be able to achieve a proper suspension in a measure, it may not be the best choice for the line overall.

Track 55

4. If you try for a suspension and then try for consonant tied notes, and neither of those options work, you are allowed to write untied half notes. If you complete a counterpoint and you have multiple places where you felt you had to include untied half notes, then you've done something wrong. A good fourth species counterpoint should have only one or two instances of untied notes.

5. In utilizing suspension patterns, you may find that you have multiple successive 5ths in the second half of the measure. Remember, in third species, we needed to have at least two notes in between perfect fifths. However in fourth species, having only one note in between is allowed, as long as no leaps are involved. Without leaps, the successive 5ths are not perceived as parallel. Including leaps makes the 5ths stand out more, providing for the undesirable parallel sound.

Track 56

As always, listen to everything. Dissonances are unstable and promote a sense of motion in the push to resolve. In fourth species, there's something special about the dissonance created via a suspension. When the pitch in the CP voice is first consonant, then becomes dissonant, it produces a unique type of dissonant motion, and can be very effective in composition.

The following are two different cantus firmi for you to practice your fourth species writing. For each CF, write a CP above and then one below the CF.

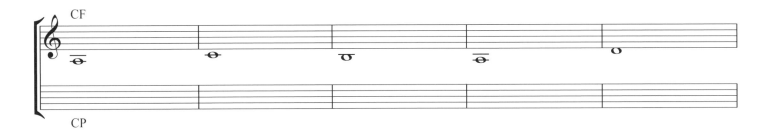

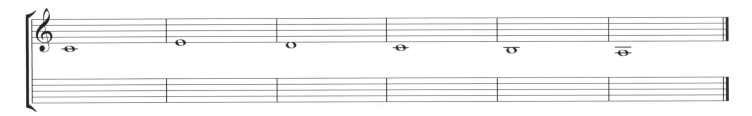

CHAPTER SUMMARY

- Suspensions occur when a pitch from the previous note or chord is hung onto while all the other notes move to the new chord and is then resolved

- First Measure:
    - Begin with a half rest followed by a half note
    - Allowable consonances are the same as earlier species

- Ending:
    - Penultimate note must end with a leading tone

- Writing:
    - Dissonances on the first beat are allowed (and encouraged), but must be resolved
    - Second note in each measure must be a consonance
    - Allowable suspensions patterns: 7–6, 4–3, and 2–3
    - Multiple successive 5ths are okay as long as no leaps are involved

CHAPTER 9: FIFTH SPECIES COUNTERPOINT – FLORID

Fifth species counterpoint is the combination of the four other species. It is nicknamed "florid," in that the combination of different species was thought to be akin to a garden of flowers. It offers more than simply combining the rules and characteristics of the other species. It is the only species to include eighth notes. This species also starts to sound like real music as opposed to an exercise.

The following are two completed fifth species exercises, taken from Johann Joseph Fux's *Gradus ad Parnassum* (1725). One includes the counterpoint line above the cantus firmus, and the other, below.

🔊 **Track 57**

Fux: *Gradus ad Parnassum,* Fifth Species with CP Above

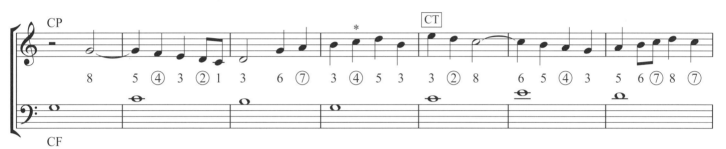

Fux: *Gradus ad Parnassum,* Fifth Species with CP Below

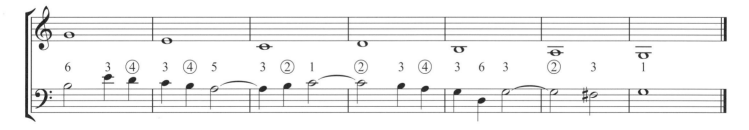

BEGINNING THE COUNTERPOINT

Begin with either second or fourth species. It is recommended you begin with a half rest instead of a half note, even though starting with a half note is allowed. Review the material on how to begin counterpoint in these two species.

ENDING THE COUNTERPOINT

Fifth species often ends with a suspension. It is the type of dissonance that works well to end a musical phrase. It is allowable to end with other species. However, do so only if attempts to end with a suspension result in the musical line being weak. To make things more interesting, you can do more to a suspension than what was allowed in fourth species. Here, suspensions may be "decorated." (This will be explained a bit later.)

WRITING THE REMAINING NOTES

Since we are now dealing with multiple different species, multiple types of dissonances are allowed. Besides circling the numbers representing dissonant intervals, please label each type of dissonance as follows:

- PT – Passing Tone

- NT or LNT – Neighbor Tone or Lower Neighbor Tone

- SUS – Suspension

For the bulk of the counterpoint, use second, third, and fourth species, but be careful not to exploit one species over the others. (The use of first species is explained later.) In fifth species, we want as much rhythmic variety as possible. Make sure your counterpoint line works on its own, characterized by all the concepts which make for a good melody. Now the rhythmic characteristics really come into play as something over that we have control. This means that part of creating a good melody involves rhythmic interest and flow. Something to consider in reaching for these goals is not to use one species for longer than two-and-a-half measures. If you get to a situation where using one species for a little longer than that makes for a good line, then it's okay, but don't do it just because it's easier to find solutions that don't break any rules.

There are specific principles involved pertaining to each species within fifth species counterpoint.

1. First species, which sees whole notes in both voices, is used only in the final measure.

2. The half note from second species should occur mostly on beat 1 of the measure. Do not include a half note on beat 2, because this rhythm forms a kind of *syncopation*, where a note gets stressed on a weaker beat or in between beats, something that is an undesirable characteristic in species counterpoint. Half notes in the second half of the measure are allowed, but they should be tied to either a half or quarter note at the beginning of the next measure. The first note in two tied notes must be a half note.

3. The faster rhythm that characterizes third species is effective in creating forward momentum. When using the quarter notes which define this species, never include "isolated pairs" of quarter notes. This means having two quarter notes anywhere in the measure where the note before and after the two quarters is a note of another value (usually a half note).

Two quarters have half
notes before and after.

So, if you start quarter notes on beat 3, the next measure should begin with another quarter.

4. Fourth species principles are the same in fifth species.

5. Eighth notes may appear in fifth species, but used sparingly, and in pairs. You can achieve this limitation by allowing for no more than one pair of eighth notes every two measures. Eighths must be approached and left by step, and occur on beats 2 or 4.

6. Eighth notes can appear as lower neighbor tones (LNT), but not upper (UNT). The lower neighbor tone can occur as either the first or second eighth note in the pair. If it occurs on the first eighth, that means that the note before the eighths and the second eighth note in the pair are the same pitch.

🔊 **Track 58**

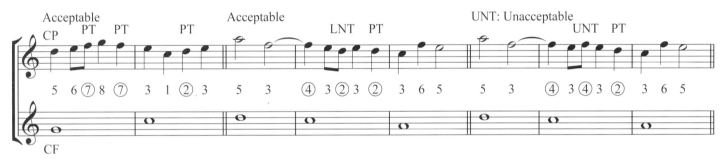

7. Suspensions in fifth species are made more interesting via *decorations*. These are created using a quarter note or a pair of eighths, and conform to the following principles:

   a. The resolution pitch of the suspension may be anticipated by a quarter note.

   b. The dissonant note may be embellished with a quarter-note *escape tone*.

   c. The dissonant pitch may be followed by a leap to a consonant interval.

   d. A pair of eighths may be used to anticipate the resolution if the second eighth note is a lower neighbor tone.

The following illustrates the principles of decorated suspensions. Notice that in all cases the dissonant pitch – which is always a half note in fourth species – is altered by turning it into a quarter note. So, in these cases, we still hear the same basic resolutions as in fourth species (7–6, 4–3, and 2–3), but with a little more activity in between the main notes of the suspension, thus existing as a decoration.

🔊 **Track 59**

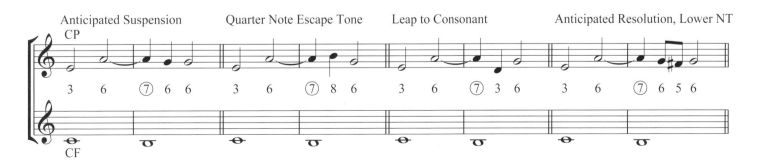

The following are two different cantus firmi for you to practice your fifth species writing. For each CF, write a CP above and then one below the CF.

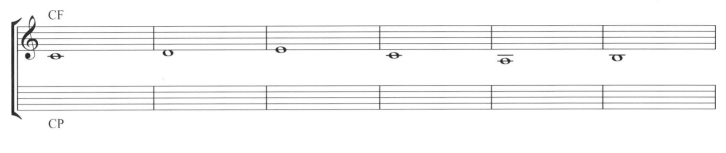

You can play your exercises on an instrument or sing them. If playing on a keyboard, try to find a sound patch that sustains notes rather than the "dying away" character of a piano. The sustained sounds will help bring out the dissonances, both when you're looking to avoid them (thus they'll stand out and you can then fix the problem) as well as when they are desired.

It is recommended you find a way to record your exercises so you can listen carefully to the results without having to concentrate on performing them correctly. When doing so, remember to listen to the lines separately as well as sounded together, in counterpoint.

CHAPTER SUMMARY

- Florid counterpoint is the combination of all other types of species
- First Measure:
    ❱ Begin with using second or fourth species
    ❱ It's recommended to start with a half rest
- Ending:
    ❱ End with a suspension
- Writing:
    ❱ First species is used only in the final measure
    ❱ In second species, use only half notes on strong beats, or in a suspension
    ❱ Do not use "isolated pairs" of quarter notes
    ❱ Eighth notes may be used, but sparingly and only as lower neighbor tones
    ❱ Suspensions can be "embellished"

SPECIES AND GENERAL ESSENTIAL CONCEPTS

The following list includes the most essential concepts of species counterpoint. While species counterpoint contains a lot of detail, the basic concepts extracted from it may be used in composing music of just about any style. Using these concepts as well as your ears, allow you to produce positive results.

- Between the two lines, use an abundance of 3rds and 6ths, but be careful not to use them in parallel motion for too long. Good counterpoint will usually see more 3rds and 6ths than any other interval.

- 5ths and octaves (and unisons) should be approached by contrary motion (in other words, no parallel P5 or P8).

- Handle Dissonances with Care:
  - Only in rare cases will there be two dissonances in a row (never involving the first or last notes of a measure).
  - Dissonances should be approached and resolved in stepwise fashion. This means using passing tones, neighbor tones (lower is preferred), and suspensions. Nota cambiata as well as decorations of suspensions, leaps involving dissonances are also acceptable.
  - Avoid dissonances on the beat (except suspensions) or in strong or accented places within the measure.

- Attempt to write contrasting rhythms between the two voices. This is referred to as *rhythmic counterpoint*. This means when one voice holds a longer note (or includes rests after a note), the other voice is more rhythmically active, using shorter notes.

- Each rhythmic line would have its own distinct identity, but both lines should work together to produce an something interesting as whole.

PART THREE:
ADVANCED COUNTERPOINT CONCEPTS

CHAPTER 10:
SPECIES COUNTERPOINT – REAL MUSIC

We will look at species counterpoint, as it applies to real music, in two ways. First, examples will be shown where it is clear to see the species rules applied. These examples will be close to species exercises, with some basic enhancements to make them more musical. After, we will look at music that more freely and expressively uses species counterpoint rules, but where they might not be easily recognized at first. These examples will demonstrate how the species rules can be used to guide and help the music, but not restrict it, as if the rules were limiting what the composer really wanted to do. This presentation is included in Chapter Eleven: Practical Use in Different Styles.

By "real music," we will be discussing two types: classical music that strictly follows the rules of species counterpoint, and modern popular music (including rock, pop, film/TV, and other styles), which may follow the rules to a large extent, but may also bend and break them at times.

This is a piano piece by the German composer Johann Anton Andrew (1775-1842). Examine the intervals, listen to the audio track (or play it, yourself), and try to discern any places where rules of traditional counterpoint have been broken. Then, listen to those spots again. Do the sounds represented by these broken rules bother you? Can you come up with a reason why the rules were broken? More importantly, how much of the time are the rules followed?

🔊 **Track 60**

J.A. Andre: "Sonatina"

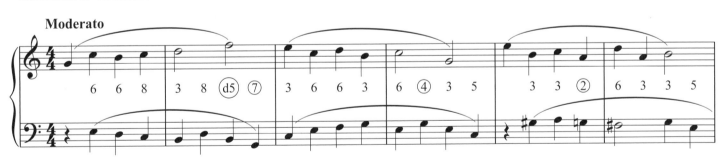

Composers do not always follow a strict set of rules. To some extent, the rules (whether counterpoint, or any other concepts in music theory) were drawn up by music theorists, after the fact. These people looked at some of the great music from the past, noticed certain tendencies, and followed. They then cross-referenced and consolidated these tendencies, coming up with these music theory concepts or "rules," based on what past composers were doing.

ENHANCED SPECIES EXERCISES

FIRST SPECIES

Examples of first species counterpoint in music literature aren't easy to find, except when they occur for brief moments. This is because one of the characteristics of good counterpoint is rhythmic independence. When the one against one ratio does occur, it only does so for a few beats at the most. Another reason is that one thing that gives music its forward momentum is the concept of tension and release, something largely created by dissonance (tension) that resolves to consonance (release). Since first species allows no dissonances, strict first species writing is not sustainable for a significant length of time.

🔊 **Track 61**

J.S. Bach: "Minuet" from *Anna Magdalena Notebook*

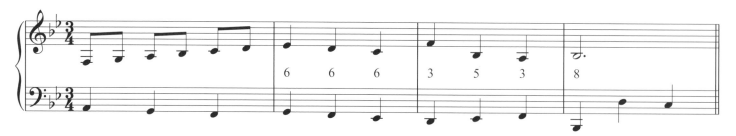

Even though first species does not allow for the necessary tension and release for an extended period between two voices, a composer can still make use of it, while creating dissonance elsewhere. For example, music may feature first species at work between a violin line and a cello line, but there may be additional voices at work, which provide necessary dissonance.

SECOND SPECIES

Species counterpoint exercises are characterized by simple ratios, such as one note against two. When we write a second species counterpoint exercise, we are writing two half notes for every whole note in the CF. In real music, it is uncommon to see something so simple and one-dimensional. With two melodies sounded at the same time, principles of second species counterpoint may come into play only for a moment during the phrase.

The following two excerpts were taken from J.S Bach's *Anna Magdalena Notebook*. Anywhere there are two notes in one voice for every one note in the other voice are spots where second species is at work (observe the places where the intervals have been written in between the staves.) The first excerpt contains no dissonances.

🔊 **Track 62**

J.S. Bach: "Menuet" from *Anna Magdalena Notebook*

The second excerpt features some dissonances. Make note of measure 4. The 4ths are not passing tones or lower neighbor tones, thus breaking strict species rules. However, since every note in the bar outlines a B major chord, these intervals are not considered unstable. Another characteristic that breaks or at least bends the rules of species counterpoint is that we see two instances of lower neighbor tones. While this type of dissonance is allowed in third species, it is not allowed in second. However, remembering that species counterpoint is characterized by strict rules regarding the writing of exercises, we see how real music allows for the bending of rules.

🔊 **Track 63**

J.S. Bach: "Menuet" from *Anna Magdalena Notebook*

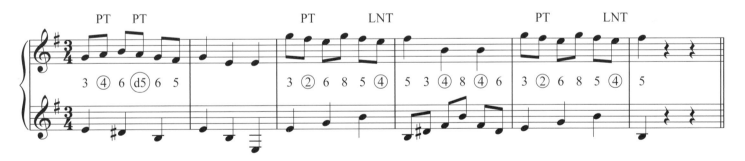

In addition, while something such as a second species counterpoint exercise has the "two against one" ratio always represented by two notes in the top voice for every one in the bottom, real music can see these roles switch at any time. In Bach's "Menuet" for example (mm. 3-6), the top voice sounds two notes for every one in the bottom voice, and then switches so that the bottom voice is sounding two notes for every one in the top, and then back again.

THIRD SPECIES

In third species, for every note in one voice, we see four notes in the other. In addition, the allowable dissonances have been expanded. You may remember that there is no species characterized by three notes against one. But in real music, this does occur, and we will consider this an extension of third species.

The following excerpt was taken from Handel's "Passepied in A Major." You will notice the distinctive rhythms throughout; however, the ratios of 3:1 and 4:1 are still at play. In the first complete measure, as well as measure 9, we again see the interval of a 4th used on the beat. However, all other instances of 4ths, as well as other dissonances, conform to species counterpoint.

Track 64

G.F. Handel: "Passepied in A Major"

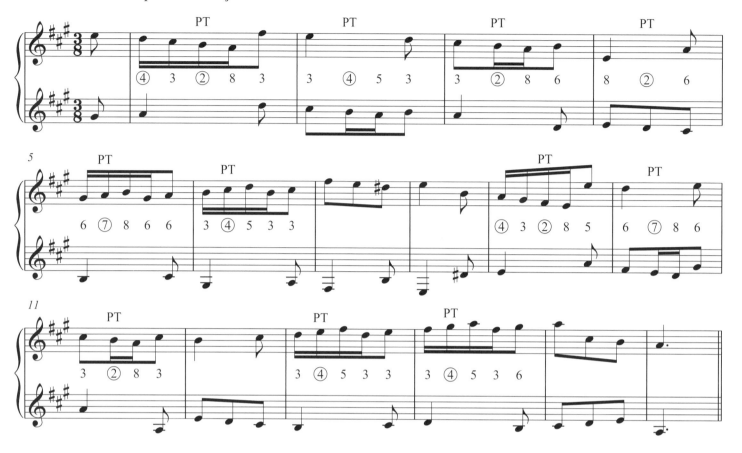

FOURTH SPECIES

Finding clear excerpts with fourth species is a more challenging task. Suspensions occur quite often, but usually not multiple instances in a row. Here are several instances of suspensions in music by some of the great classical composers.

Track 65

G.F. Handel: "Gavotte and Variation"

Track 66

C.P.E. Bach: "Allegro"

One of the most blatant use of suspensions occurs in J.S. Bach's "Invention No. 6." Due to the rhythmic characteristic, which sees two lines out of sync with each other, there is a constant series of dissonant intervals that resolve to consonant ones, with the consonant resolution occurring when only one voice changes. Also note that the perfect 4th is considered consonant. Although in strict species counterpoint, the perfect 4th was considered a dissonance, in later music, as in this Bach excerpt (from the 18th century), it was considered consonant. Since this book focuses on species counterpoint, the interval is still circled, here.

Track 67

J.S. Bach: "Invention No. 6"

FIFTH SPECIES

Since fifth species combines species 1-4, we will save illustrations of all species, combined for the next section, when we look at more nuanced examples of the basic concepts of species counterpoint.

Fifth species is perhaps best represented by those compositions where one line is expressive, consisting of many longer note values, while the other line is rhythmically active. This concept is demonstrated using the familiar "Ave Maria" by Franz Schubert in a duet for violin and cello. Chord symbols reflecting Schubert's original composition have been included. Occasionally, you may wish to write a countermelody according to a specific set chord progression. There will be more discussion on this topic in Chapter Eleven.

F. Schubert: "Ave Maria"

CHAPTER 11:
PRACTICAL USE IN DIFFERENT STYLES

The next section will see examples that use the basic rules of species counterpoint, but more freely, flexibly, and perhaps artistically. These musical excerpts will demonstrate how music that sounds less like an exercise can still hold onto these rules, using them to benefit real music.

The chapter will also explore a few additional contrapuntal techniques, where many of the principles of species counterpoint are used in different compositional strategies.

WHEN TO USE COUNTERPOINT

Depending on the style of music, counterpoint may be used as a momentary effect, such as one phrase of an entire section of music. Or it can govern an entire work, as in some of the works of J.S. Bach (1685-1750). Bach is one of the best-known composers of the Baroque era (1600–1750). The use of dense or busy counterpoint for an extended period of time may make the music sound Baroque to the average listener. (Some people hear counterpoint and simply describe it as sounding "classical.") A modern composer may wish to avoid this, unless he or she is composing a score for a film or play set in the 17th or 18th century. Less busy counterpoint, such as the vocal line against a guitar riff in a rock song, can still make use of the basic concepts of counterpoint to help it work, so it doesn't sound awkward or exhibit clashing dissonances.

Composing music is about more than simply avoiding things that sound "bad." Counterpoint can enhance certain emotions or situations in a dramatic narrative. In film, sometimes main characters are represented by musical themes in the soundtrack. Showing a relationship between two major characters can be enhanced by sounding their different themes simultaneously, in counterpoint. Sometimes, a story may depict something or someone peaceful, but hidden underneath are darker secrets. Counterpoint can be used to bring out these emotional qualities. Many stories, in film, television, and videogames, involve relationships. These might be between people/characters, places, events, etc. Counterpoint can be an effective way to illustrate relationships, since it involves two or more themes, with distinct identities, sounding at the same time, and having to work together. But relationships aren't always good relationships. They might involve danger, or some other conflict. So, two melodies might work together in a way that heightens conflict.

In addition, some of the examples in this chapter attempt to show counterpoint, within the context of a larger section. Observing these examples will demonstrate the effect of going from non-contrapuntal music to contrapuntal, then back to non-contrapuntal. Writing good counterpoint can be more than making a contrapuntal phrase sound good. It is also about *when* and *how* (or how long) to use counterpoint in the larger scheme of a composition.

While the rules seem to be aimed at allowing for as much consonance as possible, that is not quite accurate. A different perspective is that a composer should be trying to fit in as much dissonance as possible, doing so within the boundaries of contrapuntal rules. In other words, the rules indicate where something must be consonant. Outside of these spots, there are places where something could be consonant or dissonant. If a composer tries to create a dissonance everywhere a dissonance could be used, there will be measures where they just couldn't make a dissonance work. When a composer has a choice between a consonance and a dissonance, they should go with the dissonance. Dissonances that are allowable create tension and propel the music forward, without sounding wrong. If you try for a dissonance at every moment, much of the time, the rules will block you. But whenever they don't, the dissonances you add will ensure that the relationship between your lines is always progressing, full of life, and interesting.

The first example in this chapter is in the style of a classic sci-fi action film score. This is a fully orchestrated excerpt of music designed to provide an example of counterpoint in the context of a larger section, one that includes other instrumental parts besides the two contrapuntal lines. The music is meant to underscore a tense battle scene and may be divided into five short sections. At letter B, the brass delves into a phrase of strict counterpoint, making use of the following concepts:

- There is a predominance of 3rds and 6ths between the two voices.

- Whenever there is a P5th, unison, or octave, it is approached by contrary or oblique motion.

- In the second bar, the "and" of beat 1, the dissonant 4th is sounded as a passing tone. The voice does not leap to nor away from the 4th, rather it is approached by step and resolved by step.

- In the second bar, on the "and" of beat 2, we see a suspension of a 7th. This is resolved to a 6th on the "and" of beat 3.

There are more examples of the lines following the rules regarding intervals. But beyond that, each line is distinctive in its melodic interest. Play each line by itself and you will hear a clearly identifiable melody, complete with an organic contour, helped by a carefully positioned climax tone. But as is the case with some contrapuntal phrases, one melody (in this case, the top) is considered the main melody, while the other is the countermelody. Also note how sometimes both lines play the same rhythm, but for the most part, when one line holds a longer note, the other line is more rhythmically active. The same is true for the types of motion; sometimes both voices move the same direction (similar or parallel), sometimes they move in contrary motion, and other times, the motion is oblique. The variety helps keep things sounding organic and less mechanical.

🔊 Track 69

Classic Sci-fi Action Film Score Battle Scene

Next, we will take the main melody (trumpet) from the previous example at letter B and create a different countermelody underneath. This new countermelody will be like the previous example, but will break some of the rules of species counterpoint. You be the judge as to which one sounds better. Also, take a moment to compare the two versions and make note of where the rules were not followed.

🔊 **Track 70**

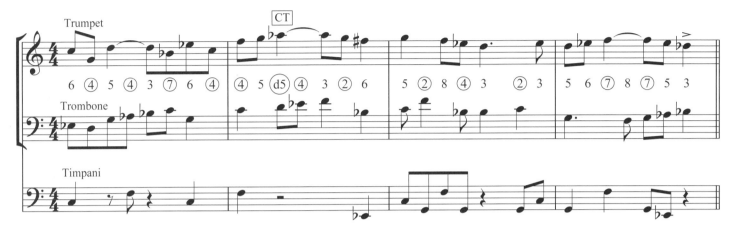

Notice some of the violations:

- Numerous instances of dissonances that are sounded at inappropriate times, such as being leapt to or leapt away from.
- Some dissonances are sounded on strong beats.
- There are instances where two dissonances occur in a row.
- Perfect intervals are arrived at via similar motion instead of contrary.
- There is no climax tone (the highest pitch is F, but it occurs twice).

If one were unaware of the rules governing traditional counterpoint, and tried things out "by ear," to create a countermelody to accompany the top, this is what might result. Does it sound bad? Maybe not. But one could argue that it could be better. In a situation such as this, if the composer learned some of the rules of traditional counterpoint, they could take this example and alter the countermelody to better conform to the rules. Knowing the rules ahead of time and using your ears in combination with knowledge can produce better results more quickly.

As previously mentioned, following the rules (as if you have them in front of you, opened to the appropriate pages of this book) can produce positive results. But this can still seem like you're not being as creative as you want to be. Perhaps it feels much like you're still creating exercises for a class. If you make it a regular habit of completing species counterpoint exercises as a warm-up to composing, you will internalize the rules, and they will become an automatic part of your creative ear. Some composers spend fifteen to twenty minutes a day, creating one species counterpoint exercise. Eventually, you will find yourself creating satisfying contrapuntal music more quickly, and doing it in a way that feels natural, because you're following these traditional rules without thinking about them and carefully keeping track.

While traditional counterpoint deals with two or more equally prominent melodic lines sounded at the same time, many of the concepts governing counterpoint may be extended beyond that setting. For example, one melody may be considered the main melody while the other is in a supportive role. Being supportive may mean it is not quite as interesting on its own in some way. Extending this further is the concept of a melody sounded with a bass line. The bass line might be simple compared to the main melody. Another situation involves a melody sounded with an ostinato or riff. A riff is often short and repeats itself several times in a row. The riff may be sounded four times while the main melody is sounded only once and spans the length of the four repetitions of the riff. In these situations, the concepts involving intervals between the two lines may still be useful, even when one of the lines is clearly more simple or repetitive than the other.

The next example illustrates the concept of a repetitious guitar riff, underneath a melody that is different through the entire length of the riff pattern. The bass supports the guitar, playing most of the same important notes (octaves apart). Between the two, there are no dissonances, just a lot of 5ths, so it has no tension. This writing technique makes the guitar sound bigger. However, there is some counterpoint to it, as there are a few 3rds and 6ths. Three-voice counterpoint is an advanced concept, even though many of the rules are the same. That is a topic for another time, but you'll get a small taste of it with this rock excerpt. (Note: Guitar sounds an octave lower than written.)

 **Track 71**

VOCAL COUNTERPOINT

The following example is in the style of a famous classic rock song. It is two-voice counterpart, consisting of three voices singing the lines. However, the three lines do not sing at the same time; rather, one voice takes over when another drops out. The three intersect for just one note. The same excerpt is presented twice: once with analysis, so you can see the rules of counterpoint at play, and one with the lyrics. On the audio track, the excerpt is played two times, with Voice 1 in violin, Voice 2 in viola, and Voice 3 in cello. The first time through is just Voice 2 (viola) by itself (with bass and drum set). The second time is all voices.

 **Track 72**

There's one thing different about this example, compared to the previous examples. It was composed as counterpoint between multiple singing voices. One challenge with vocal counterpoint involves the lyrics. Independent voices, even when singing the same basic lyrics, can muddle in terms of the listener being able to understand the lyrics. In music from hundreds of years ago, vocal counterpoint was a big part of a lot of church music. In this liturgical music, congregations knew what words were being sung.

With a rock tune, someone hearing the song on the radio may wish to be able to hear the lyrics clearly. But even with songs that don't involve vocal counterpoint, we all know that isn't often true. The songwriter has to determine how important it is that all lyrics are understood. One could write their counterpoint, attempting to make the lyrics heard as clearly as possible, or accept that it may be difficult, and rely to some extent that the listener will obtain the lyrics in text form, perhaps online or in the liner notes for the album.

The following example shows our vocal counterpoint song, with the lyrics included. You are encouraged to sing the parts, to hear how well both lines of lyrics can be understood. Either grab a partner to sing with you, or record yourself singing one of the parts. You may wish to transpose the excerpt if it does not sit comfortably in your vocal range.

MELODY ABOVE BASS LINE

As mentioned previously, the rules guiding traditional counterpoint refer mostly to melodic lines that are less than a 10th apart. However, when dealing with greater separation between two voices, using traditional species counterpoint rules is still useful in helping you create two lines with a solid relationship, where each individual line helps the other, making the combination of the two lines greater than the sum of the parts. One thing to note is that if a melody is at least a couple octaves above the bass line, this may mean there are other notes in between the two lines. These other notes may consist of pitches to help fill out chords and thicken the texture. Some of the following examples will demonstrate these thicker textures, while others will keep that space in between the two voices vacant of other pitches.

With good counterpoint, a composer can create something sounding full, with just two voices. This next example is in the style of the theme from a well-known science fiction television series. This was created simply, with a distinctive bass line and a melody above it. While it is clear that the top voice is the main melody, the bottom voice, while being accompaniment, is still distinctive on its own. When creating a piece of music, sometimes a simple accompaniment part such as a riff or bass line becomes one of the main hooks. People remember this just as well as the melody. This example is in line with species counterpoint concepts, where the composer is directed to make each individual line interesting by itself.

Because the bass line is distinctive, it may be that it was created first. Even though you might have music with a main theme, it doesn't always mean that the theme was created first, and then the composer wrote the other parts around it. Sometimes, a songwriter creates something such as a bass line and then is tasked with coming up with a melody to be played over the top of it.

The following are a couple additional points of which to take notice in this example:

 * Leaps of an octave are generally not considered leaps, rather a change in orchestration. Octave leaps can be a useful tool to take a melodic line suddenly much lower or higher. In addition, they can affect the type of motion that follows. In this case, the change in octave allows the following 5th to be approached by contrary motion. If the line had remained in the upper octave, going to the E on beat 1, the next measure would've resulted in the 5th being approached by similar motion, something that is frowned upon in traditional counterpoint.

 ** This big leap is not something you usually see in music following traditional rules. However, it is done here for a special effect. This example sees the use of large leaps as an identifying characteristic of the theme. If something like this is done on an instrument that can easily execute it, the leaps can be effective in making the melody more interesting.

The next example is in the style of a famous classic TV theme from an adventure series. This example features an ostinato in the bass with a melody sounding above it. There are several dissonances that don't conform to traditional rules. However, they occur on the same beat within a repeating (but slightly varied) motive in the top voice. This repetition helps make the dissonances build in tension towards a resolution at the end. Sometimes, a dissonance repeated in a similar way multiple times, becomes a motif and is justified.

There are five spots marked by asterisks, where at least one rule is broken.

> * In the third bar on the "and" of beat 2, the long note in the top voice provides tension and dissonance. An interval of a 7th is created between the top voice and bass line; however, due to the staccato articulation in the bass note, the A and G are not actually heard at the same time.

> ** The F♯ in the top voice forms a dissonance when the bass sounds a C on the "and" of beat 4.

> *** On the "and" of beat 3, the top-voice note forms a dissonant 4th with the C in the bass.

**** The augmented 4th is not an interval allowed in traditional counterpoint, at least when it occurs on the beat. But if you look at measures 7, 8, and 9, you see the repeated figure in the top voice gradually travelling down by half step, on beat 2 of each measure. This traveling, along with the dissonances, are building tension to measure 10, when we get a resolution on a tonic (an A minor chord).

***** Like the previous measure, but now the 4th is perfect. It is arrived at by leap, something that is against the rules. If you put the preceding E (on the "and" of beat 1) in the melody up an octave, then the dissonant 4th is approached by step and resolved by step. This would make it an "accented passing tone." This is a case where the composer should use his/her ears to evaluate a breaking of the rules. You could try changing this in various ways to conform to the rules, and perhaps something better would result. But if not, go with the version that breaks the rule. When evaluating something like this, always put it in context, meaning back up at least a few bars to start your listening and continue through until a couple bars after the questionable spot.

USING COUNTERPOINT FOR REPETITION AND VARIATION

Composition relies on repetition. A songwriter, when writing Verse 2 can use the same music and include different lyrics. Musically speaking, this would be *literal repetition*, which is anytime something is repeated in the exact same way, or very nearly the exact same way. A well-constructed song will be based around two or three main ideas that get repeated and varied (or developed) in different ways. If a composer tires of the monotony of too much literal repetition and wants greater variety within a song, there are ways to take an idea and repeat some aspect surrounding the essence of that idea to make it sound different. Depending on how this is done, listeners may pick up on that fact that something is being repeated, and perhaps marvel at the creative skill behind making that happen. Or, listeners may not notice on a conscious level that something is being repeated, but the repetition seeps into the listener's subconscious, making the song appealing, and giving the listener the desire to hear the song many times in the future.

Counterpoint is just one of many devices that can be used to repeat core ideas and give the listener something different and unexpected.

INTERWEAVING MONOPHONIC AND POLYPHONIC

In the following example, we see the guitar and bass playing the same line, an octave apart for one phrase. Then, while the bass repeats this melodic line, the guitar plays something in counterpoint. This is an effective use of repetition and variation. In pop/rock songs, often the music in the verses is the same, with just the lyrics changing. But sometimes instrumentally the second verse will have a subtle change compared to the first. For example, the first verse might see the electric guitar playing with a clean (no effects) sound, and then in the second verse, the guitar plays something similar, but this time using distortion.

The organ line adds color in the upper register, above the guitar and bass. Whether it's playing chords as in the first eight bars, or a single-note line as in the second half, it is playing notes that the guitar and/or bass are already playing. Still, it could be considered a third voice in the counterpoint. (Note: there is some rhythmic counterpoint in the organ, as heard in the "back and forth" between it and the guitar/bass). When you create two-voice counterpoint, and wish for another instrument (or more) to play something else at the same time, you have the option of constructing something from what the two contrapuntal lines are playing.

INVERTIBLE COUNTERPOINT

Invertible counterpoint is a way of composing two voices, where the top melodic line is repeated in the bottom voice, and the bottom line is moved to the top voice. This means that if you have a guitar line above a bass line in counterpoint for a four-bar phrase, when you repeat the phrase, you have the guitar play what the bass played and the bass play what the guitar played. The roles switch but the guitar is still above the bass. For the first example to demonstrate this, we'll use the familiar tune "America (My Country 'tis of Thee)."

 **Track 76**

"America (My Country 'tis of Thee)"

One of the challenges in writing counterpoint that can also be inverted without breaking the rules, is in the intervals of the 5th and 4th where the former is considered consonant and the latter dissonant. If you write a 5th between the two voices, when you invert the lines, that 5th becomes a 4th. If you do this, you'll need to make sure the resulting 4th follows the rules regarding dissonances, in that it functions as either a passing tone, suspension, or lower neighbor tone.

The next example, *Swan Lake* by Pyotr Ilyich Tchaikovsky, features a challenge in that the melody doesn't follow the general prescription for what makes a good melody. Much of the time it is simply arpeggiating chords. Tchaikovsky's melody is in the top voice, while the countermelody is in the bottom. In addition, soft chords in the strings help fill out the arrangement.

🔊 **Track 77**

Tchaikovsky: *Swan Lake*

Note how, in measure 5, there is some *chromaticism* (pitches outside the key). On beat 3, whether the bottom voice plays G♯ or G♮, both form the interval of a 3rd with the top voice. This is something you can experiment with, especially if you want to be adventurous and add extra flavor to your music.

Now, observe the same counterpoint inverted, with the same soft chords in the strings. See and hear how the inverted lines can be used when other parts remain the same.

Tchaikovsky: *Swan Lake*

* While this is technically a diminished 4th, enharmonically is it a 3rd. Think of the F spelled as an E♭ or C♯ spelled as a D♭.

Take note of the last three bars: there are a lot of 3rds and 6ths in a row. This is because Tchaikovsky's melody is arpeggiating chords, displaying a lack of stepwise motion. Doing this for too long, especially when both voices are arpeggiating chords at the same time, can sound less like melodies, and more like accompaniments. Great melodies don't always follow a certain prescription. What might be perceived as flaws can be what makes music more magical. So, a challenge in attempting to write counterpoint with a melody such as this, where the line often outlines chords, is trying to include dissonances, those "tension and release" moments that help propel the music forward.

Now, you might be asking yourself: why would a composer desire to write counterpoint, dealing with two lines that could be inverted, and still not break any traditional rules? When you create melodic lines, especially main themes, you want to repeat them throughout the composition, putting them in different settings and variations. If you create two lines, where the top voice is a main theme, that means you can repeat this theme in a lower voice/ instrument, and still use the same exact countermelody, but in a different, higher instrument. Melodic lines can be like characters in a story, and composers, like storytellers, want to be able to use these characters throughout the story, while keeping them well-defined, and not having them take certain actions that are "out of character." When characters in a story don't stick to a certain identity, they become less distinctive. Invertible counterpoint is one way you can maintain a close relationship between two lines.

SEPARATE MELODIES WORKING TOGETHER

Melodies that are played or sung separately, at different places in a composition, could be constructed to eventually work simultaneously. For example, the melody used in the verse of a song and the melody from the chorus could be sounded at the same time in the bridge of the song. Or, if themes represented certain characters in a video game, when these two characters interact, the music could sound the two themes in counterpoint.

This can be a tricky endeavor. A composer wants to create a great catchy melody for each character, themes that have strong hooks. Trying to first create two melodies that work well when sounded together in counterpoint may involve a sacrifice in how strong and catchy they are when sounded separately, in different sections or settings of the game.

One option is to create separate melodies, with the goal of making them into strong hooks in their own sections, not worrying about how they might sound when played at the same time. Then, to sound them together in counterpoint, allow for variations in the melodies, preserving as much of the original melodies as possible, so that they are still recognized. Doing this in the bridge of a song is acceptable and even desired. The bridge can often exist as a *development* section, one where themes, motives, riffs, chord progressions, and other elements from the song are repeated and varied in different ways, as if main characters in a story are going through challenges, adventures, and other experiences where they learn, grow, and change. In a video game, different settings and situations, but with the same characters, allow for variation and development of the melodic themes.

The following example shows two individual melodies, which may serve as to represent two different characters, or simply the A and B sections of a composition.

🔊 **Track 79**

Notice that the melodies are in different keys, as is standard in the A and B sections of a composition, and is also the case sometimes between the verse and chorus of a song.

Next, we transpose one of the melodies to put it in the same key as the other, then see what they look and sound like together. The A melody has been transposed down an octave in order to put some distance between it and the B melody. However, you could try transposing the A melody above B, and see what works best.

Track 80

Writing in the intervals, we see quite a few problems with dissonances in inappropriate places. In addition, there are some parallel perfect intervals, as in the parallel 5ths in measures 1 and 5, and the final two bars, where perfect octaves occur four times in a row.

This is not a bad sound in that it does not clash. However, you lose a sense of two distinct lines whenever parallel intervals occur. Listening to the example confirms the troubled spots. The task is to fix these problems, while retaining the essence and distinctive characteristics of both melodies. Alterations can be made to either melody or both. Pitches or rhythms (or both) may be changed in order to achieve this. Once you have something that looks good, play it back to make sure it sounds good. Remember, you're not just going for counterpoint that doesn't have problems, you want something that attains the type of sound you're looking for. The following is one possibility.

* Spelled as an aug 2nd, which is enharmonically equivalent to a minor 3rd.

In this version, measure 2, on the "and" of beat 3, we have a 4th that is leapt to and away from. If there is a traditional counterpoint rule broken, but it sounds good to you, try fixing it. Then listen to it compared to the version with the broken rule. Sometimes fixing a broken rule will improve something even if it sounded good. But if the broken rule version sounds better, go with it. Then, make note of what rule you broke and how it was broken. You could use that facet in your writing elsewhere, and it may help unify your composition. Some broken rules will sound worse than others. With our "modern ears," something such as a 4th, executed in a way that breaks a rule, does not sound as bad as it did to listeners 300 years ago. With that in mind, in measure 1 beat 4, and measure 5 beat 4, it was decided to leave the parallel 5ths alone. Our modern ears are used to hearing these, and a couple instances of them is not enough to take away from the perception of two independent lines.

Finally, we set these melodies within an orchestrated section, where other instruments help support the themes. As has been mentioned before, just two lines in counterpoint can provide thickness and denseness to the texture. When adding other instruments, be careful not to overdo it, or the music will become muddy and cluttered. If the two contrapuntal lines are close together and somewhere in mid-register territory, then one option is to write other parts that are very high and/or very low. In addition, other parts can highlight some of the same notes and rhythms as the contrapuntal lines. This can help punctuate and bring out certain rhythms.

In choosing to employ counterpoint in a situation like this, you can also try setting the melodies in different keys from each other. You will usually get the friendliest sound by using one melody in a key closely related to the other. The first choice is to go up a perfect 5th from the first key. For example, when one melody is in A minor (no sharps or flats in the key signature), the other melody could be in the key of E minor (one sharp key signature). Or, if the second melody were down a 5th, it would be in D minor (one flat key signature).

CHORD PROGRESSIONS AND COUNTERPOINT

Composers may wish to write counterpoint according to a specific harmonic progression. In a composition dealing with more than just two instruments/voices, it may be that other instruments are playing chords, and you will want your countermelody to adhere to these chords. Take note that, when writing counterpoint according to pre-determined chords, it is neither necessary nor practical to have every note strictly adhere to the chord progression. Follow as closely as you can, then evaluate the counterpoint. Listen to these lines along with the chords, and make decisions based on how it sounds to you. If this is your own composition, you have the freedom to change the chords based on the counterpoint. Some of your decisions will depend on the orchestration, especially how much vertical space there is between the counterpoint lines and the instruments playing the chords. You may have chords being sounded in between the two contrapuntal lines, above the lines, beneath them, or a mix.

For the next example, we will use another familiar tune in the theme from Antonin Dvořák's "Largo," which is the second movement in his *New World Symphony (Symphony No. 9)*. Here, the chords are sounded in between the contrapuntal lines. If you write something like this and are having trouble with things sounding too cluttered, you could move the top melody up an octave, the bottom melody down an octave, or both.

NOTE: While the main melody is taken directly from Dvořák's symphony, the countermelody, sounded in the bassoon, was created for this book.

 Track 83

Dvořák: "Largo" from *New World Symphony*

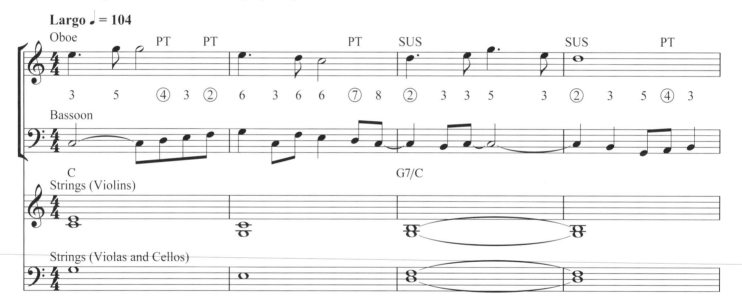

Chords are often a part of popular music, so the next example is a rock tune. If you write rock music, you may find yourself in a situation where you or the guitar player in your band come up with a great guitar riff. You are then tasked with creating a melody to go on top of it. This could be a vocal or instrumental melody. To keep things simple, we will say that the bass plays the same basic line as the guitar, but an octave lower, something very common in rock music. Then, let's say you think of a nice chord progression to be played on a clean electric guitar along with the distorted electric guitar riff. Individual composers as well as multiple members of a band often come up with ideas for different instruments and voices, and in different orders. It's great practice to adapt and create something that works well when played with any other type of idea.

🔊 Track 84

While the melody is sounded in a synthesizer, it could be a vocal melody. Vocal melodies are often simpler than instrumental melodies. A melody for the human voice tends to have fewer leaps and more stepwise motion. If you are creating a melody you think could either be sung or played on an instrument, it is best to keep it simple and try singing it yourself as you compose.

In addition, you may have noticed that there is only one dissonance in this rock tune (m. 8). Due to the simpler nature of the top melody, the repetitious guitar riff, as well as the arpeggiated chords in the clean guitar, this is acceptable. As an exercise, try creating your own top-voice melody to go along with the other parts and attempt to create more dissonances.

Besides creating counterpoint according to a chord progression, a composer could work in reverse to this procedure. Once a contrapuntal section has been created based on the notes sounded simultaneously, at certain important moments, chords could be created utilizing those notes. For example, if the two voices sound a C and an E at the same time, a C major chord could be used. Important moments might include beats 1 and 3 (in 4/4 time), or any place accented by syncopated rhythms. This is one way to add additional instruments to a section featuring two contrapuntal lines.

CHAPTER 12:
ADVANCED TECHNIQUES

The final chapter serves as a brief introduction to more advanced contrapuntal concepts. If these are of interest to you, it is recommended you continue your counterpoint studies beyond the book.

IMITATIVE COUNTERPOINT

If you've ever sung "Row, Row, Row Your Boat" as a round, then you are familiar with *imitative counterpoint*. It is characterized by the same melody being sounded in multiple voices but out of sync. A round is also known by the term *canon*. Let's look at this tune to see what kinds of intervals result when one melody is sung out of sync with itself. The second voice is sung an octave below the first.

 **Track 85**

"Row, Row, Row Your Boat"

We see two dissonances, with the first one being a proper passing tone, and the last one a 4th, but not conforming to the species counterpoint rule regarding 4ths. One thing about 4ths is that they are not considered dissonant when there is another voice beneath the 4th an octave below the top voice. For example, if in measure 8, we put a G underneath the bottom voice, it would stabilize the 4th between the top two voices. Another thing to consider is that the 4th is not perceived as a dissonance in modern music, at least not as much as it was in classical music of the 18th and 19th centuries.

You can choose when you want to start the second voice. "Row, Row, Row Your Boat" saw the imitation begin after the fourth bar. With the total length of the melody being eight bars, that means the first half of the melody will have to "work" when sounded at the same time as the second half. Having the imitation begin at a half-way point through the melody is common and a simple way to begin your first attempt.

You can begin by creating a melody that's an even number of bars in length, let's say four. Then, write the melody four bars out of sync with itself, and see where problems arise, if any. Let's say you came up with the following.

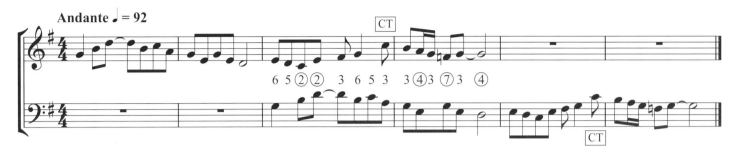

Just by listening, you can hear that there are some problems. So, write in the intervals and see if that tells you where the problems are. In this case, we see that in one instance we have two dissonances in a row, and other dissonances don't conform to the rules of species counterpoint. The trick in dealing with this is that you don't simply want the melodies to work together with respect to the dissonances. You also want this melody to be interesting and catchy. In addition, look at any perfect intervals to make sure they are approached by contrary or oblique motion.

Leave the first two bars alone, thus only dealing with the top voice in measures 3 and 4. The bottom voice is playing the first two bars of the melody, which began in the top voice, so that needs to stay the same. Change notes and rhythms so that the two voices work together at the overlapping point. The following is one example of some changes that work.

Track 87

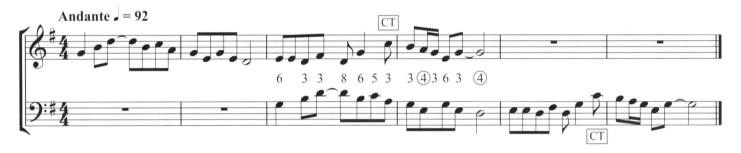

As you study the changes, notice that the 4th, which ends the imitation, was left alone. It may sound unstable, especially if there were no other parts being played along with these two lines, but at least the pitches belong to a G major chord, and this example is in the key of G major. After this, copy the last two bars of the top voice (the ones you just changed) into the last two bars of the bottom voice, so the melodies match.

If the piece were to continue, in measures 5 and 6 of the top voice, you could create something new that goes along with the bottom voice. This technique of imitative counterpoint could be used for just a phrase here and there, within a composition. Perhaps it gets used as an effect in a pop tune, occurring just once. Imitative counterpoint doesn't have to be the basis for the whole composition, rather just used in small doses. If you were to utilize imitation as the main element on which to create the work, this would be a type of music called a *fugue*. There are entire classical works, or single movements which are fugues. J.S. Bach was just one of many composers to create works of this genre.

CHROMATICISM AND ATONALITY IN COUNTERPOINT

TONAL, BUT CHROMATIC

Much of the epic orchestral film and game music – especially those from the sci-fi, fantasy, and adventure genres – have its roots in music from the Romantic era (c. 1827–1900). While the music was tonal, it made heavy use of *chromaticism*, where pitches from any given key were altered. While a piece in the key of C major is based on the pitches of the C major scale (C, D, E, F, G, A, B, C), other pitches outside these seven were used to provide for a wider variety of harmonic options, as well as melodies that saw a greater potential for color. Since the Romantic era was largely based on the idea of music expressing emotions, stretching outside of any one key, while still remaining in that key, chromaticism allowed the composer to express a wide variety of emotions. A melody that is strictly in the key of C major (using no pitches outside the major scale) could be harmonized by chords that exist outside the key. In addition to these options, Romantic works would change key more often, providing a degree of ambiguity as to what the key is at certain moments.

Chromaticism is a useful tool in conveying not only a variety of emotions, but also a diverse array of settings. Even though a melody may frequently delve outside the pitches of the given key, the rules of traditional counterpoint can still be adhered to. The following excerpt is in the style of an adventure film or game, with an expressive chromatic melody. The key is C major, but just at a quick glance, you'll notice an abundance of accidentals. Chord symbols have been included to help illustrate the harmonic progressions that move beyond chords belonging to C major. While the main melody is sounded in the violins, the countermelody is sounded in the cellos and basses. Notice that the countermelody follows the rules of traditional counterpoint, even considering the chromatic nature of the excerpt.

In addition to demonstrating two melodic lines in counterpoint, this example fills in some of the other voices based on chords, to provide a thicker texture. You might ask yourself whether you'd first compose the two lines in counterpoint and then construct chords to accompany these lines, or create a melody, harmonize it with chords, and then create the countermelody based on the chord progression. The answer would be "yes," meaning you could tackle this task either way or in combination of both methods. You could create a melody, then harmonize that melody. As you work on creating the countermelody, attempting to follow the chord progression you designed, if there's a choice with respect to counterpoint that goes against one or more of the chords, you could simply change the chord. There is no one single method for creating a section of music in this style. There are two audio tracks for this example. The first track plays just the melody and bass line, while the second plays the full orchestral arrangement.

Track 88

Track 89

A few notes about this example:

* In the first measure, this may be perceived as a parallel 5th. You be the judge on how this broken rule sounds.

** Here is a dissonance not resolved by step, rather by minor 3rd.

*** In measure 13, this is the climax tone of the melody, which is rather late. However, some melodies rise as they proceed, saving a climactic moment for the end. In addition, G♯ above C is technically an augmented 5th, which is the same as a minor 6th. So, in effect, because of the chromatic nature of the melody, we have two different 6ths in a row.

POLYTONALITY

While not common in rock and pop music, the use of *atonal* (non-tonal) structures has a useful place in music for film and videogames. The unresolved dissonances often associated with atonal music offer effective sonorities to help portray anything tense or scary in these stories, as well as a host of similar moods and situations.

A melody that is not based on the pitches of the major/minor scale or the church modes, rather some other type of synthetic scale or a chromatic collection of pitches, can sound atonal and thus dark and scary on its own. However, given a tonal melody, other techniques may be employed to add a certain dark and tense quality to it, with respect to counterpoint. *Polytonal* music is that where two or more different keys are at play at the same time. One common type of polytonality is *bitonal* music, where two different keys are sounded simultaneously. When dealing with two-voice counterpoint, this is achieved simply, where one voice could be in the key of A minor, thus using the pitches of the A minor scale, while the other voice could be in C♯ minor.

With respect to counterpoint, the rules of traditional species counterpoint still govern everything. The intervals of 3rds and 6ths are the imperfect consonances that occur the most in traditional counterpoint. However, there is no difference between a major 3rd and a minor 3rd with respect to the allowance of this interval, and the same goes for 6ths. When dealing with bitonality, one can still make use of the same interval distances as if it were a tonal section of music, but in many cases, the interval quality would be changed, thus giving it the atonal, or at least more chromatic, sound. Perfect intervals would still have to remain perfect. For example, while a perfect 5th is a restful consonance, a diminished 5th is a dissonance.

The following example takes the familiar melody "Greensleeves," in the key of E minor, and uses a countermelody in the key of G sharp minor. This technique may be appropriate in film/TV music, where something more peaceful has a darker undertone.

 **Track 90**

Greensleeves

Using two different keys simultaneously produces different interval possibilities. You may also notice that, because of the mix of accidentals, some enharmonic curiosities occur. For example, measure 3 sees two 6ths in a row. Enharmonically, the A♯ is the same as B♭, so between that pitch and the upper voice G is a major 6th, while the following B against G is a minor 6th. If enharmonic spelling isn't your strong suit, use your ears to judge. While something bitonal can sound unconventional, if following the rules of counterpoint, you shouldn't hear any clashing dissonances at inappropriate times. If you hear something, check the spellings and double check the intervals.

Bitonality provides for atonal structures that are still clearly and simply organized. However, one can still follow the rules of traditional counterpoint while dealing with melodies that are not tonal.

SYNTHETIC SCALES

In atonal music, the concepts of consonance and dissonance take on different meanings. In some atonal works, all intervals are treated equally, meaning no interval is considered stable or unstable. Still, this is not always the case. In utilizing synthetic scales, a composer can follow the same rules regarding consonance and dissonance as in tonal music.

The following is in the style of early 20th-century impressionist composer, Claude Debussy (1862-1918). It makes use of the *whole tone scale*, a six-note scale with each pitch separated by whole steps. This example follows the same rules of consonance and dissonance as in traditional tonal music counterpoint. To help enhance the impressionistic style, suspensions are the favored type of dissonance.

Finally, the last example makes use of the *octatonic scale*, a collection of pitches favored by 20th-century composer, Béla Bartók (1881-1945). The scale sees alternated half and whole steps to produce an eight-note scale. While counterpoint rules regarding dissonance are generally followed, this example has made the interval of a tritone (diminished 5th or augmented 4th) a consonant. It is the interval that dominates the composition, much in the style of some of Bela Bartok's works.

In the following example, note that some instances (such as measure 1, on the "and" of 4) are spelled as an augmented or diminished interval, however labeled enharmonically as their consonant counterparts (A5 = m6).

Track 92

"Tri This!" (In the style of Béla Bartók)

You are encouraged to delve into more 20th-century classical music, where other very different concepts of counterpoint make up a variety of interesting compositions.

CONCLUSION

Writing counterpoint can be a painstaking task, but the results are worth it. Contrapuntal composition is possible in any style of music where there are two or more voices. While some styles are not known for counterpoint, that doesn't eliminate the possibility of including it. Music must evolve, and trying something that is considered uncharacteristic of a certain style may make for just the right element to create something new and unique.

Jazz and blues tunes often consist of a melody and chord progressions around which the instruments improvise their parts. In improvisatory music of this style, counterpoint is challenging. If a player knew exactly what the melody was playing, it is possible to improvise a good countermelody. However, two instruments, both improvising make for a tricky task in creating effective counterpoint. Still, there are plenty of jazz tunes that include sections of composed parts that do include counterpoint.

Whether you're composing classical, rock, pop, film or video game music, counterpoint can help you explore many possibilities with your melodic ideas. It can also add a certain amount of sophistication and complexity to your work. What was presented in this book offered the most basic and traditional concepts in writing counterpoint, but these are by no means hard and fast rules, nor are they the only methods. These concepts provide a good start, and should you continue to explore them in different ways, they will go a long way to helping mature your own compositional identity.